MW01528849

CONTENT THAT CONVERTS

The Ultimate Guide to Building Authority, Establishing Trust, and Creating Lifetime Customers

CONTENT FIRST MARKETING

The Ultimate Guide to Building Authority,
Establishing Trust, and
Creating Lifetime Customers

John Arnott

Clear Again Media, LLC

Copyright © 2014

Content First Marketing

Performance Publishing Group, McKinney, TX

All Worldwide Rights Reserved, McKinney, Texas

All rights reserved. No part of this publication may be reproduced, stored in a retrieval system or transmitted, in any form or by any means, electronic, mechanical, recorded, photocopied, or otherwise, without the prior written permission of the copyright owner, except by a reviewer who may quote brief passages in a review.

ISBN-13: 978-0-9906553-3-6

ISBN-10: 0-9906553-3-4

TABLE OF CONTENTS

PREFACE

This book is the result of several years of learning digital marketing the hard way. I spent so much time, blood, and sweat understanding what works and what doesn't that it only seemed appropriate to get it in writing and share it with others.

Since building my first business in 1997, I have always considered online marketing as a cornerstone to a well-formed marketing strategy. While times have changed and tools and techniques have evolved, there are some tactics that have proven the test of time. Giving something of value to a prospect or customer, building authority and expertise in a specific area, and earning trust are the key components to creating lifelong customers. The challenge we face today is doing this in an increasingly noisy environment.

Getting beyond the noise and being heard is the marketer's objective. I intend to walk through each of the key digital marketing components and show how they are used and how they fit together so that you can manage your own digital marketing efforts.

This book will cover writing with authority—including the lost art of copywriting headlines. I will address building trust with email and social media as well as such advanced tactics as retargeting and marketing analytics.

Authoring a book like this has been challenging and rewarding. There is a certain challenge in sharing what works when digital marketing changes daily. There is great reward in finding those techniques that will endure. The writing process has helped me as a marketer to evaluate tools and channels with an even more critical eye in an effort to provide the best advice.

For the past 15 months, I have tested each of the techniques in this book for relevancy.

Thank you to John Arnott, Sr., without whom I could not have completed this project. I would also like to thank my wife, Daisy, for her never-ending support and my mother, Ellen, for supporting me throughout my life. Finally, I would like to thank my sister, Michelle Prince, for her guidance on the writing and publishing process.

Sincerely,
John Arnott, II
2014

INTRODUCTION

Some people will tell you that it is no longer possible to market a business successfully online. They believe that Google's algorithm changes have made it impossible to make your business visible or that your site will never be seen in a saturated market. I'm here to tell you that this is not true.

The fact of the matter is that online marketing is here to stay. As long as people have problems, they will always need creative solutions and products that will make their lives easier. There will always be a demand for high-quality, informative content, and the people who can fill that demand will never hunger for customers.

In *Content First Marketing*, I am going to give you some tips and strategies for growing your business. I will teach you some solid strategies for generating high-quality content, gaining visitors, converting those visitors into loyal customers, and encouraging viral growth of your brand. This is a book of ideas that is meant to inspire you, but it's also a book of solid, actionable advice that you can put to work immediately.

Content Strategy

The focus of much of this book is on content creation. High-quality content is the key to successful online marketing, which is why I preach the value of "content first marketing." Content is what will bring visitors to your site, what will keep them around to learn more about your products, and, especially, what your visitors will share in order to bring more traffic back to your site. The value of web content cannot be understated.

Creating web content for your site, however, isn't as easy as simply stringing keyword phrases together, despite what some outdated Search Engine Optimization (SEO) practices might have taught. In this book, and in my own business strategies, my focus is first and foremost on high-quality, informative content. Here are a few reasons for this:

- High-quality content is naturally keyword rich. When you write authoritatively about a topic, you cannot help but use the exact keywords that someone interested in the topic would use in a search. This will naturally boost your search engine rankings without needing to artificially inflate your keyword density.
- High-quality content is shareable, which increases the likelihood that it will go viral. When you publish great information, people will naturally want to share it with their friends and family. Every time someone shares your page, you get free publicity and widen your sphere of influence.

Most importantly, high-quality content is safe from

future changes and modifications to the algorithms used by Google and the other search engines. So-called "black hat" SEO tactics can get fast results, but those results are not sustainable. A website built on tricks and cutting corners will be rendered useless by search engines as soon as the exploits and loopholes are solved.

So, with that in mind, my content strategy is one based on purely "white hat" tactics. In other words, I recommend that you build your website around Google's best practices. By working within the rules laid out by Google, you ensure that your site will live a long life and will not need constant rebuilding to keep up with the newest trends. In this book, I will teach you how to achieve exactly that—and more!

What This Book Covers

Content First Marketing is divided into nine chapters, and each chapter is divided into sections. You do not have to read the entire book in order, but I think you will get the most value from it if you do, because every lesson builds on concepts developed in the previous section. Some chapters are information-dense and packed with ideas, so you may want to refer back to them often once you've begun building your own content-rich website. You might discover that some of the ideas I present in this book make more sense after you've tried putting them into action for yourself.

Here is what you can expect to see in this book:

- First, I'll address creating a product worth selling. This is the cornerstone of your business, and it's something that you can easily lose sight of when you get caught up in creating content and marketing your website. Your product is the end-game of your site, the object toward which you are ultimately driving buyers. Chapter One will help you actualize your ideas to create a killer product.

- After that, I will devote several chapters to address content. I'll go over a few tried-and-true strategies for writing content like an expert—this is the key to a high ranking among today's sophisticated search engines. I will also teach you how to write compelling sales copy, focus on headlines, and use the power of psychology when crafting your message.

- A great product and solid, valuable content make up the core of any successful business, but you will not start reaping benefits until you have promoted the site. After I address how to master content creation, I will present the best strategies for building organic traffic, which includes gathering valuable backlinks and using social media to your advantage.

- I will also explain how you can use your mailing list and special retargeted advertisements to stay in touch with your prospects and create more conversions. This is a crucial piece of information that many marketers don't know about when they're first starting out, so pay special attention to these chapters—they will give you a serious advantage over your competition.

- Finally, I will focus in detail on the value of analytics, how you can monitor your behavior and what that information means. As you will soon learn, analytics is a crucial part of any marketing agenda. Learning how to analyze your company's performance will help you succeed in your endeavors.

If you are ready to get serious about your business, I can help you grow your sales. By the time you finish this book, you will be well on your way to becoming a pro at "content first marketing."

So what are you waiting for? Let's get started!

1 PRODUCT OFFERING

The Internet has been a game-changer in the way that products are marketed and sold. Over the past decade, online sales have tripled, accounting for approximately seven percent of the total sales realized in 2013—amounting to over $27 billion in purchases. The reach of online sales goes even further than that since many customers now discover and research products online before buying them in a brick-and-mortar store. In the future, it is highly likely that online sales will continue to grow as people become more comfortable with virtual shopping and businesses start offering more products through the Internet.

There are some companies that have carved out a corner of the Internet market and made amazing profits from it. These sites started out just like yours. They have landing pages, calls to action, product descriptions, and an online shopping cart. Why is it, then, that some sites routinely rake in high profits while others languish in obscurity?

Several factors affect the success of an online business, including marketing, and even pure luck. But the one thing that every highly successful online business has in common is that they are all selling products that people want to buy. Before you can expect to make money with your business, you need to identify your audience and determine *... product packaging and development is the crucial first step to digital marketing.* what products will speak to their needs—then you encourage them to buy from you. This is why product packaging and development is the crucial first step to digital marketing. Everything else you do will flow from the product you sell.

Knowing What to Offer

The first thing to bear in mind when planning your offerings is that they should be composed of different types or levels of products. This is especially true if you plan to sell high-end products or services. In these cases, it becomes necessary to attract buyers with smaller offers as a way of establishing trust and authority. Once someone has purchased a smaller product from you, he or she may be more willing to invest in a pricier option.

With that in mind, you will ultimately want to think of your business as offering three things: a core product, an engagement product, and a lead magnet.

Core Products

Your core product is the main thing that you are trying to sell. It should closely align with the purpose of your site and the overall vision of your company. This is true whether you're selling something of your own design or another person or company's product through affiliate marketing: Any product that you sell should match the website you sell it through.

The reason for this should be obvious. If you are a consumer looking to buy smartphone accessories, you wouldn't think of buying them from a website about organic fruit. You would look for a site with the focus of its content on electronics and smartphones. You would assume that a company that seemed knowledgeable in a field would also sell quality products.

I will address establishing your expertise in your niche further on, but for now just remember that your core product represents what your users are ultimately going to get out of interactions with you. In other words, an athletic shoe store may sell numerous different types of sneakers, but every pair of shoes it sells exists to be worn under athletic conditions. The store's core product is athletic footwear, and it offers many modes of delivery for that product.

Engagement Products

An engagement product, also known as an introductory product, is something that helps to attract buyers to your business. If you are selling fairly low-priced products through your site, an engagement product may not be necessary. If you're planning to sell high-priced products or services, however, the engagement product is a crucial aspect of building trust with your visitor.

Think of it this way: You would probably not be willing to pay $1,000 for a six-week class from someone you've never met or heard of before. However, if you have read a few of the person's books on the topic and find that his information is valuable, you will be much more motivated to try the class. In this example, the books serve as engagement products.

There are two key components to creating a successful introductory product. First, it must have a low enough price point to be enticing—frequently between $7.00 and $17.00. Second, it must have the perception of added value. For example, someone buys one book from you and receives a second book for free, boosting the overall value of the offer. This makes the enticement product irresistible. Once you've hooked the buyer with your introductory offer, you will probably

> *There are two key components to creating a successful introductory product.*

see repeat business, as long as that first offer delivers what the visitor was hoping for.

Lead Magnet Products

Sometimes, your visitors need more than a little incentive to start doing business with your company. An introductory product may not be enticing enough to secure a buyer. In these cases, you will want to offer a free lead magnet as well.

The lead magnet is a free product that you offer to entice people to sign up for your mailing list. Using our earlier example of the $1,000 course and the $17.00 book, the lead magnet might be a free 10-page report on the topic. This might be a totally original report, or it could be a chapter from the book you're selling. In either case, the crucial qualities of the lead magnet are that it's free and it matches the core product of your business.

Once you have secured an email address, you can stay in touch with your subscribers. Through your newsletter, you can offer coupons or other special offers to encourage people to buy your products. You might also notify subscribers about new or upcoming products. That way you might capture the interest of someone who did not need something you were selling a month ago but might be very interested in buying this new product.

Think of this in terms of a sales funnel that captures the interest of prospects and gently guides them toward a purchase. You will secure many more valuable customers this way than if you offered only your high-end core product.

Identifying Your Niche

At this point, you may already know exactly what your core products are and what you could offer for introductory engagement offers and lead magnets. If so, you're ahead of the game! If not, though, don't get discouraged. There are several ways that you can go about finding the perfect product offerings for your company.

> *There are several ways that you can go about finding the perfect product offerings for your company.*

Where Does Your Authority Lie?

When brainstorming product ideas, you will first want to determine what niche you occupy and what authority you might have. If you already have a website or blog in place, you can look to your existing content to determine where you have already established authority. You can then create a product based on that information.

For example, imagine that you have a recipe blog. You could easily use that as a way to sell cookbooks, meal-planning services, or private cooking lessons. Readers would be likely to trust your advice and ideas because they have already seen the quality of information on your blog.

To determine where your authority lies, there is a handy

tool called AlchemyAPI. This is a website that allows you to examine your webpages and blog posts for keyword taxonomy—in other words, how your keywords fit into existing categories. These categories will be displayed to you with increasing specificity, with broad categories at the top and more specific ones at the bottom. This allows you to pinpoint your niche.

Start by visiting http://www.AlchemyAPI.com and choosing "Try Our Demo." Then select "Alchemy Language." Copy and paste the text you want to analyze, then hit return. The results will show you your keyword density and the top categories for each post.

This information is important because it allows you to see what market you inhabit and who your competition within that market may be. Looking at your competition allows you to see what products they're selling so that you can come up with a few ideas of your own.

Scoping Out the Competition

Once you know what keywords and categories your website falls into, you can begin searching for similar sites. First, do a quick Google search and view the top 10 websites, give or take, in any given category. Then, look at what products they sell, including the introductory offers and lead magnets. Make note of what you find before moving on to the next site.

This research can take several hours—or even days—so try to stay organized by putting together a simple spreadsheet. By documenting the site, its category, the keywords, and the products sold there, you can have a quick reference for your own product development.

Finding Out What's Popular

Simply knowing what other companies are selling can be hugely helpful for choosing your own product offerings.

> *... you will be most successful if you learn to identify what products are in high demand.*

However, you will be most successful if you learn to identify what products are in high demand. Otherwise, you run the risk of offering a product that no one is searching for and missing a valuable opportunity elsewhere.

One great way to see which products are trending and which have passed their prime is by looking at sales trends among affiliate marketing groups. Of course, these trends will be limited by the types of products a particular affiliate sells, but it can be a powerful jumping-off point. Here are a few sites to visit for inspiration:

Clickbank

CJ (formerly Commission Junction)

Plums

Amazon

AffiliateBot

Click2Sell

These are all popular affiliate product providers and are used by many online businesses. They act as a go-between for companies selling products and the websites that market them, acting as matchmakers between the two. Affiliate companies gather large amounts of valuable data about the behavior of any given product, and you can easily view trends to see what is selling today and whether something is gaining or dropping in popularity.

For example, if you visit the Clickbank website, you can navigate to the "Marketplace" page. Once there, choose the category that most closely matches the category of your own site. This will bring up a list of available products and services within that market. It will also provide relevant information about the recent trends affecting those products, including sales price.

The statistic you want to pay the most attention to is called "gravity." This refers to the number of affiliates who have earned a commission in the last 12 weeks from selling that product. If a product has a high gravity, it means that it is popular and in demand.

There are a few other ways to spot emerging trends in product offerings. Many search engines offer a service for identifying trends. Try Google's Zeitgeist or

Yahoo's leading searches. You might also want to check out Amazon's "Movers and Shakers" list for more inspiration.

Standing Out

By this point, you should have a solid idea of what products are being offered by competitors within your niche. Your next goal is to conceive some product ideas that will be different enough to stand out from the competition. After all, you don't want to produce something that already exists elsewhere; you want to use what you know about the market to identify gaps that can be filled by your offerings. Ultimately, you want to find a product that exists in the sweet spot between "what people are looking for" and "what other groups are already selling."

> *Ultimately, you want to find a product that exists in the sweet spot between "what people are looking for" and "what other groups are already selling."*

If the product you have in mind does compete directly with something another company is selling, ask yourself a few questions:

- Are your products interchangeable, or is there something that makes one inherently more valuable than the other?
- Is price the dominant factor when determining which product to buy?

- Have you already exhausted your opportunities to trim production costs?
- Are profit margins already dangerously slim?

If your answer to one or more of these questions is "Yes," you may exist in the red ocean of price competitiveness.

Differentiating Yourself in the Ocean of Red

The red ocean of price competitiveness refers to a market where the only thing distinguishing one product from another is price. This is not a place you want to be, as it quickly becomes unprofitable. Competition turns into a race to the bottom, and profit margins evaporate.

The way you stand out from your competitors in the red ocean is by adding value to your products. Think of it this way: At the grocery store, there might be an entire wall of sandwich bread. For most consumers, white bread is white bread, regardless of who's producing it, so they will simply pick the cheapest loaf. However, if your bread is made with high-quality ingredients, such as organic flour or exotic grains, you can afford to charge more. People who will spend $1.00 on white bread will happily put down $4.00 on a loaf of exotic, organic bread.

Look at your potential product offerings to determine if you can come up with a few ideas for adding value. By offering something that nobody else offers, you allow yourself to stand out from the competition and rise above the red ocean.

Product Definition

By this point, you have completed a lot of market research and should have a good idea of where you stand in the market and what types of products might be most successful. Now, it's time to narrow down your list to determine what core product your business should sell and what introductory offers and lead magnets you may be able to offer that will complement it.

If you will be creating a product rather than selling another producer's wares, now is the time to determine the exact specifications of what you'll be selling. It is also the right time to make a plan for producing it and delivering it to your buyers. If you know exactly what it is that you're selling, you will have a much easier time marketing it later on, so don't rush this step. Take the time necessary to explore every facet of your product offering before it hits the market. There are many things you will need to consider:

- What problem does your market face?
  - o What solution are you offering?
- What "pain points" or specific problems does your product solve?
- What are the most important benefits of your product?
- What consumer need does it fill?
- How much will it cost the customer?
  - o How are those costs assessed? Fixed, variable, recurring?

- Will you sell it online, over the phone, face-to-face—or some combination of the three?
- What options will come with it, and how will those affect pricing?
- Are there installation or maintenance requirements that need to be considered?
- Who is your primary competition?
- What additional products, such as introductory offers, would complement the core product?

Answering all these questions will lead you to develop a solid product offering, allowing you, your team, and your buyers to know exactly what you are selling. This product offer makes up the core of your marketing efforts, as all marketing materials will highlight the information you uncover during this step. It is also crucial for creating and delivering the product as it allows the company to create exactly what you have in mind. Your product definition stage is not complete until this product listing process has been finished, so take some time with this before moving on.

Sales Testing

Before you begin heavily marketing your products, it's a good idea to test them. You will soon discover that testing is an integral part of every step of business growth, and choosing a product offering is no exception.

Launch your site with your product offerings in place,

and see how well they do. You might want to try split-testing at this point: Create two different versions of your site, each one selling slightly different products, and see which version gets the most interest from buyers. This is especially important with your lead magnet and introductory engagement offers as these need to appeal to the widest number of visitors. Anyone who becomes hooked by these offers becomes a prospect for your core products, but you might not capture as many prospects as you want if you have the wrong lead magnet.

Once you have tested your products and begun to get the sort of results you want, it's time to move forward with your marketing plans to widen your audience and attract the attention of many more prospects.

Your Final Offer and Looking Ahead

Identifying your product offerings can be time-consuming, but it is well worth the effort to do the research in advance. Starting a business with a solid set of products builds a great foundation for your future.

As time goes on, you may find that you will need to change your product offerings. This is natural and beneficial. You will especially want to swap out your lead magnets and introductory engagement offers on a regular basis. A visitor who may not have been interested in a previous offer may be especially intrigued by your new offers, which in turn will lead to a prospect and even a sale.

Once you have become comfortable with the products that you sell, it's time to start looking toward your long-term marketing plan to develop strategies for growing your business. This is how a small website grows to become a powerfully lucrative online marketplace.

A visitor who may not have been interested in a previous offer may be especially intrigued by your new offers…

2 WRITING AUTHORITATIVE TOPICAL ARTICLES USING RELATED KEYWORDS

As Google continues to update its search algorithms, webmasters everywhere are struggling to keep up. The sharpest among them have realized what others have yet to discover: Search Engine Optimization (SEO) as we know it is dead. The old tactics for getting your work recognized and rewarded by search engines have stopped working. In many cases, these formerly safe SEO practices can now result in your site actually being penalized and losing rank. This shake-up is huge, and it has left many webmasters scrambling for answers about how to create the content that Google wants to promote.

The good news is that while old SEO tactics no longer

> *... instead of crafting content that will appeal to search engines, your goal should be to create content that will be meaningful and valuable to visitors.*

work, your page rank is not left to chance. You can control how well your pages perform in searches by modifying your content. In this regard, SEO is still alive and well. But now, instead of crafting content that will appeal to search engines, your goal should be to create content that will be meaningful and valuable to visitors. Sites that succeed doing that will continue to do well, gardless of what changes occur to search engines in the future.

In this chapter, I will address the details of crafting authoritative content. First, I will show exactly what authority means in the context of building webpages. Then I will demonstrate how the concept of a "good" page has changed, thanks to the evolution of searching and SEO practices. After that, I will get into the details of crafting the kind of high-quality content that will bring visitors to your site and boost its ranking.

Google Values Authoritative Content

Google uses a sophisticated system for identifying whether a site is valuable. It ranks sites according to their authority. In other words, Google will give priority to sites that are written by experts or that provide expert-level information. From the perspective of a user, this makes sense: If you were looking for information on a topic, you would want to know that the information is correct, valuable, and not something that you already knew through common sense. To improve the user's experience while browsing, search engines now place the highest value on authoritative websites.

SEO Practices: Then vs. Now

The goal of search engine optimization is to land your website in the first page of search results for a given topic. In the past, the first question a webmaster would ask was, "How can I get my site on page one?" Today, the first question should be, "Why does my page deserve to be on page one?"

"Why does my page deserve to be on page one?"

The primary purpose of a search engine is to connect users with the best response to a searcher's inquiries. If you want to find information about boats, for example, you might go to Google and type "boat" in the search bar. Google would then look for all the webpages that have the word "boat" in them and return them, ranked in order, so that those that seem most relevant or valuable come up first.

In the past, the relevance of a page was determined by its

keyword density. In other words, a site that had the word "boat" written in it frequently must be a good source of information about boats. For years, this is how search engines worked, but it was a system that could be easily abused.

In the past, building a successful website was a matter of optimizing that site for search engines. In a way, the search engine was your primary audience, and webmasters designed their pages accordingly. Today, writing for the search engine is a recipe for disaster. You must write content with the user in mind. When you write content that is useful, interesting, and share-worthy, it will also be valuable from an SEO perspective.

When search engines found and ranked sites based entirely on keywords, obtaining a highly ranking site was simple. A webmaster simply needed to identify a keyword that was popular and build a site around that keyword. The word or phrase would be placed in several vital places, like page headings and the opening paragraph, and the text surrounding that phrase would be largely irrelevant.

Now, thanks to updates in Google's search technology, searches look at more than keywords. In fact, the search algorithm is designed to identify a searcher's intent rather than the exact words typed into the search bar. The exact phrase used matters less than the general topic surrounding that phrase.

Today's search engine optimization is based on building

up a site's authority. Authoritative websites are judged on several factors:

- The links back to a website. If a site is linked frequently by other trusted sites, it stands to reason that it must be a reputable, authoritative source of information.
- The sites it links to. If a website links out to high-value, authoritative sites, it is reasonable to expect that its content will also be well-researched and of high quality.
- The exact vocabulary used. Experts writing about a particular topic will by necessity use specific vocabulary related to that topic. The presence of these niche words is what Google uses to identify the content of a website.

While all these issues are important, the final point is what I will focus on in this chapter. Learning how to use niche vocabulary is an important skill for webmasters, and it's one element of your site that you have total control over. In the next section, I will look at what exactly niche vocabulary is and how you can use it to lend an air of authority to your website.

How Google Determines Authority: A Look at Niche Vocabulary

When an expert writes an article about a topic he is familiar with, that article will automatically contain certain words. These words are essential to the topic, and they work together as related keywords to convey the meaning of the article to the search engine.

For example, someone writing an article about car insurance would likely use words such as "deductible," "collision," "coverage," "claim," "liability," and "risk." These words are necessary to explain the topic of car insurance. As such, you can be sure that any high-ranking article about car insurance will include most or all of these words.

Similarly, specific topics within a niche will have their own specialized keywords in addition to the general niche vocabulary. For example, an article about filing an auto insurance claim will include most of the words above, but it would also most likely include terms such as "adjuster," "inspection," "at-fault," "repairs," and "estimate." Again, this is because these are words that are necessary to discuss the topic at hand.

Every topic will have its own related keyword groups. Before I examine how you can identify the niche vocabulary for a given topic, the most important thing to remember is that understanding how to use related keywords will lend an air of authority to your site and boost its quality while also improving your page rank.

Utilizing Related Keywords in Your Writing

What is important to remember about keyword clusters is that they cannot and should not be used like regular keywords. If you set out to write an article that contains as many of the related keywords as possible, your endeavor will likely fail. Niche vocabulary must arise naturally from the topic that you are writing and your expertise about that topic. In other words, you need to start with the topic first rather than amassing keywords and trying to write text to fit around them.

With that in mind, by far the simplest way to create a high-authority webpage is to have an authority to write it. If you are already an expert in a given topic, you will naturally use the kind of related vocabulary that Google can identify and use to rank your page. If you are not an expert, you could find one to write your article for you. This is the model behind many successful websites, such as WebMD or About.com. Experts are hired to provide content within their particular niches, and all that content is pulled together into a single site by the webmaster.

Depending on your situation, this may not be possible. You may not have the connections or budget to hire a team of experts to create the content for your website. Fortunately, it is possible to write like an expert without actually being one. This will require some research and effort on your part, but it's a worthwhile endeavor if you wish to create high-quality content that will earn a high page rank and invite ample traffic from visitors.

Tools for Identifying Niche Vocabulary Words

When you are planning content for your website, you will

> *... there are several tools you can use that will help you pinpoint related keyword ideas and identify niche vocabulary.*

want to make sure that the site offers information that is relevant to what people are searching for. You will also want to make sure that the vocabulary you're using on the site is consistent with what experts will use when discussing those same topics. Fortunately, there are several tools you can use that will help you pinpoint related keyword ideas and identify niche vocabulary.

Clear Again Media

Clear Again Media offers a free tool for doing related keyword analysis. You can find it at http://contentfirst. marketing/related-keywords-tool/

The related keywords tool begins with an article. You enter a base key phrase for the article. The tool will then search Google for the top 10 articles for the base key phrase. It then extracts common words and phrases from these articles, filters out common words and lists the words and phrases sorted by frequency. You now have a list of niche vocabulary words for your article. Once your article is written, you can paste it into the article window and the related keywords tool will analyze the usage and display a density map. Finally, it will run the article through a plagiarism checker and provide a score.

SEOquake

A valuable tool for any webmaster is SEOquake, a toolbar and browser add-on that will provide useful insights into pages throughout the web. It works with Firefox, Google Chrome, and Opera, and you can use it to learn all sorts of things about the pages you see, including their page rank and keyword density.

SEOquake also offers a helpful tool for identifying niche vocabulary. To use it, identify a high-quality website in your niche. Use the SEOquake "keyword density" tool. This will automatically pull up and highlight recurring words and phrases. Make note of what these phrases are. When you go to another page in the same niche and analyze its keyword density, you should come up with a very similar list. Analyzing several high-quality websites within a given niche should give you a very clear idea of what related keywords are essential to discussing a topic.

You can use SEOquake's keyword analysis tool to spot the difference between high-quality and low-quality websites within a given niche as well. Simply run a keyword analysis on an authoritative, well-respected page; then run the same analysis on a page on the same topic that does not rank as well. You will see quickly that the related keywords prevalent in the top-tier results will be lacking in the lower quality sites.

Using SEOquake on your own website or page will help you identify the keyword density and measure it against well-respected sites in your niche. This can help you see whether you're on the right track and whether you need to make any vocabulary adjustments.

LSI Keyword

LSI stands for "latent semantic indexing." This is one of the most popular tools for identifying related keywords and phrases. You can input a specific topic and receive keyword lists for single-word, two-word, and three-word keyword phrases that frequently appear together in clusters.

One of the most useful elements of LSI is the ability to search for keyword phrases within specific Google rankings, so you can easily use this tool to compare the phrases in the top result against those in the top five or 10 Google results. This can help make it clear what the general related keywords are and what words might be more specifically related to a particular website.

In the past, LSI Keywords and its related service, ThemeWriters, was used to create targeted articles for SEO purposes. The idea was to identify several valuable keywords and cram them into an article to boost a page's rank for that keyword. Today, this type of keyword stuffing will cause more harm than good.

Instead, you should look at LSI Keywords as a tool for inspiration. Rather than trying to stuff a list of keywords into every piece of content you write, you should look at the listed words and phrases as a whole to see what relationship they have to one another. Use this to inspire your own content by giving you an idea of what major points should be addressed within an article on that topic.

Google AdWords

If you have experience with SEO, you are probably already familiar with Google AdWords. Officially, the point of this program is for businesses to utilize the targeted advertising system, AdSense. AdSense works by identifying the words within a page and displaying advertisements based on the content of the site. For example, a website about car insurance might display ads about accidental injury lawyers or vehicle repair shops. A website about dogs might display ads for dog breeders, trainers, or pet food vendors.

AdSense functions on exactly the same technology as Google's web searches. The program views a page, identifies particular keywords and phrases, and then determines the site's topic from that information.

As a webmaster, you can take advantage of this. To make AdWords work for you, you will need to go to the "Keyword Planner" tool. Select the option "Search for new keyword and ad group ideas." Type the topic of your website or page into the "Product or Service" field, and leave everything else blank. Click search.

What you will receive is a listing of what words are related to that primary keyword and what people are searching for on a regular basis. In the past, you would use these keywords to build a website. Now, you will take a more indirect approach: Instead of using these words exactly as they are displayed, you will look at the general trends among searches and use that to guess at the intent of people searching. Once you know what people are searching for, you will have a clear idea of what you can offer that will be valuable to them.

Once you have written a webpage, you can go back to AdWords to review your keyword usage. Return to the keyword planner. This time, instead of typing in a keyword, place the URL of your new page in the "Your Landing Page" field. Leave the rest blank. Click "Get Ideas," and AdWords will generate a list of keywords targeted at the content of your site. If these keywords and phrases match the niche vocabulary that you are trying to use, you have succeeded. If not, you will need to go back into your article and tinker with it to ensure that you're using the right words to let Google know what your page is about.

How to Write Like an Expert

The process of writing like an expert is a matter of research. First, you must identify the niche vocabulary within a given topic. Next, you must determine what all of those words mean and how they relate to one another. Then, you must craft content that will speak naturally to the topics encompassed by that niche vocabulary, keeping in mind the needs of your audience.

If you are already well versed in a subject, writing authoritatively about it should be pretty simple. You would just sit down with a topic and explain it naturally, using the vocabulary necessary to discuss it. For example, if you were going to talk about health insurance, you would probably explain the difference between an HMO and a PPO; you might talk about deductibles, out-of-pocket costs, coinsurance, and copays. These are all related keywords that arise naturally in a discussion of health insurance, and you would use them in your explanation of a topic.

However, imagine that you didn't know anything about health insurance, but you need to produce a high-quality website about health-care coverage. To do this, you must research the topic. This is where the keyword tools from the last section come into play.

First, find a few sites written by obvious authorities on the topic. For health insurance, this might include the website of a major health insurer or a government health

department site. Next, run an SEOquake on the site to identify the related keywords used in the site. Make a note of
common words and phrases that are repeated throughout.

Now review this list of words and phrases and make sure
that you know what they all mean in context. If you are un-
sure of a word or phrase, look it up. You need to use these
words correctly in order to convey useful information to your readers,
and using keyword terms inappropriately will result in poor search engine
performance.

... you should also have a pretty firm understanding of the basic concepts behind the topic you're writing about.

Once you have a general idea of what the keywords mean, you should
also have a pretty firm understanding of the basic concepts behind the topic you're writing about. At this point, if someone were to ask you to explain
this topic to them, you could do a reasonable job at relaying
accurate information.

Put this knowledge to work by identifying what people
are actually searching for. Using your list of keywords, start
dropping a few important keywords into the AdWords keyword planner as described earlier. This will bring up a list of
actual searches that people are doing.

A search on health insurance, for example, will turn
up a number of searches, such as "buy health insurance,"

"health insurance plans," and "cheap health insurance." Based on that, you can reasonably assume that most of the people searching on the topic of health insurance are looking to buy an affordable plan. Your goal, then, is to create a webpage that will provide relevant information about that topic: Address what affects health insurance costs; explain the difference between different types of plans; give tips for trimming insurance costs.

When you have finished your page, you can run it back through AdWords or SEOquake to make sure that you are including the correct vocabulary. You will also want to review your page for writing quality, paying attention to style, grammar, and the quality of information. Before publishing a page to your site, ask yourself whether you could see it at home in a glossy magazine or large newspaper. If not, your quality is not high enough to beat Google's ranking system.

Saving Time

If reading the above advice makes you nervous, don't worry. In the beginning, your research and writing will be more time-consuming. However, many of the steps outlined above will become unnecessary as you gain comfort with the material. After all, you will not need to look up what the important keywords and phrases mean after you've done it the first time. From that point on, you can focus the bulk of your research on identifying what your readers are searching for so that you can deliver it to them.

In effect, this new method of SEO is really just a process of becoming an authority. Even if you do not have personal experience in an area, you can speak authoritatively by looking at what others have said.

Of course, it's easiest to become an authority on a topic that you are already experienced with or at least very interested in. If you have not yet begun building your site, you should give some thought to your topic of choice. Now more than ever, choosing a niche that you are comfortable writing about at great length is a crucial component to success.

A Note about Outsourcing

If you are not comfortable providing this high-quality content yourself or are simply uninterested in spending your time on this project, it is possible to out-source this task. Many of the same article-writing sites that once provided keyword-rich content for SEO experts have shifted their focus to catering to expert-level writers. For example, My-Bloggerz.com offers cost-effective, authoritative article writing on a subscription basis.

You will end up paying more for this content than you would for low-quality SEO-type writing, but you will also need significantly less content than before as there will be no need to place hundreds or thousands of articles throughout the Internet for backlinking purposes. It is up to you to review your budget and decide whether hiring an experienced writer is a better use of your resources than putting the time into writing your own articles.

Regardless of who is doing the actual writing, it will be your job to identify what content should be created. Whether you are writing it yourself or giving it out as an assignment, you will need to know what your audience needs and how you intend to deliver it to them.

Putting It All Together: Writing Content People Want to Read

So far, you have learned why writing authoritatively is so crucial to success in the current SEO climate, and you have seen some tactics for identifying and using related keywords in order to boost the quality of your site. In this section, I will go over some more specific details on writing the kind of content that will attract readers and enable your site to flourish.

Coming Up with Ideas

The goal of writing for the web in today's environment is to write for readers, not for search engines. This means that your topic choices should be guided by the needs of your customers or readers. As I explained previously, simply looking at the searches that people make involving certain keywords can yield tremendous insight into what people are looking for. There are a few other ways to tap into the needs of your readers directly:

- Question sites, such as Quora or Ask.com, often yield valuable insights into what questions people may have about any given topic. Find questions that seem to be popular but that have no other satisfactory answer online, and write articles that will answer those questions. You can also join those question sites yourself and offer advice through them, boosting your own credibility as an expert and giving you the opportunity to share links back to your site as appropriate.

- Forums abound for topics in a variety of niches. Join a few forums related to your topic and pay attention to what questions are asked often or what problems seem common. If you can offer an article that will answer those questions or provide solutions to those problems, it will be very valuable to readers in your niche. You can share links to your content on these forum sites as well. Just be sure that you also spend time chatting there and simply socializing or being helpful rather than simply dropping links.

- When a blogger in your niche posts a controversial topic, consider writing a response from the other perspective and linking it in the comments. Controversial articles are more likely to attract readers, and this allows you to continue the discussion in a way that provides value to readers who are already invested in the issue.

These should give you some ideas as a starting point when it comes to brainstorming topics. By combining the knowledge and vocabulary of an expert with the topic ideas in highest demand from your readers, you can ensure the highest possible quality for your web content.

Going Viral As a Standard of Quality

Today's Internet is highly social. Content is shared by individuals through their social media profiles in addition to their emails, instant messaging programs, and forums. This means that today many people are not discovering their websites through search engines. Instead, they are finding them through links left by other Internet users. Therefore, it is your duty to ensure that your site is optimized not just for search engines but also for sharing among users.

Basically, your goal with any piece of content that you create should be to make something people will want to share. To do this, you will need content that is high-quality, trustworthy, and authoritative. It will also need to offer something that cannot be found else-

> *Basically, your goal with any piece of content that you create should be to make something people will want to share.*

where.

Some types of content are more readily shared than others:

- List-format articles that deliver information in bite-size chunks. Lists of facts and trivia are particularly valuable as people find them interesting and are more likely to remember them than if the information were delivered in another format.

- Quizzes and other types of interactive content. Users like to share their results with friends and compare notes. Use this to your advantage when thinking of ways to design your content.

- Tools that are useful to visitors. These might include guides and how-to content or tools that can be used in daily life.

- Images, videos, sound files, and other multimedia methods for conveying information quickly and in an entertaining manner.

- Content that is controversial and thought-provoking will do better than content that takes a more neutral stance.

When you are looking for content ideas for your website, look around at the social media profiles of your friends and family. This should give you a very good idea of what people are most likely to share or be interested in. You can also view the social media presence of your competitors within a niche. The most successful sites will have content that invites sharing and virality.

Standing Out from the Competition

If you have done your research correctly, you have undoubtedly discovered that many other websites cover your topic in an authoritative way. Depending on your niche, competition might be fierce for top-ranking search engine results. Given this competitive environment, you need to be creative in your approach so that you can guarantee the success of your content.

Building content that readers will want to share is one major piece of the puzzle. It does not matter how well your competitor ranks in search engines if you are getting more visitors each day through social sharing. The links generated by all that activity would raise your rank naturally.

The other method for outranking your competition is to present the information in a new way. Use your research to discover what questions are not being answered fully, and strive to provide a more thorough response. Give your content some personality and relate to your readers on an individual basis.

For example, imagine that you are writing an article about dog training. You have used the tools discussed above to identify the niche vocabulary and see what people are searching for. Now, take the very best bits of information that you've gathered from other sites in your niche, and present it in a more interesting manner. Try to really get inside the mind of the person who will be searching for your content. Instead of writing the article, "How to Train Your Dog," write it from a different angle: "Why Does My Dog Keep Chewing My Sofa?" or "How Do I Get My Dog to Stop Barking?"

These are exactly the types of personal questions that people are increasingly likely to type into search engines. Using "I" in the headers and titles creates an immediate personal bond with your reader, and infusing the information with personality will help it stand out from the crowd. Keep asking yourself every step of the way what your reader wants to know and how to best deliver that information.

Final Words

In many ways, search engine optimization has become much more complicated since Google became more sophisticated. In other ways, however, writing successful content has actually become easier. You no longer must find a way to squeeze irrelevant keywords into your articles or spam backlinks across thousands of websites in order to draw readers to the page. All you have to do is write high-quality, interesting, authoritative content that answers readers' questions. This is certainly not easy, but it is simple, and it will become easier with practice.

The best part of approaching SEO in this way is that it's

a method that is unlikely to change. Although the details of search algorithms may change in the future, search engines will always want to connect users with the most relevant information. By striving to provide the information that your audience wants and needs, you can create content that will weather Google's future updates.

3 HEADLINES THAT SELL

Copywriting is the cornerstone on which any good marketing message is built. The words on the page do more than describe a product or service: They compel a person to action. Good copywriting is what converts a prospect into a customer—and it is often what draws those prospects in the first place. Even if you are not a professional copywriter yourself, you can still put some of their strategies to work when designing your company's message, whether it's putting together your website or designing an ebook to hook readers.

One of the most crucial parts of the copywriting message is the headline. A few short lines of text can have a powerful impact on a reader. A good headline is what makes someone decide to stay and read

> *One of the most crucial parts of the copywriting message is the headline.*

what you have to say rather than scroll past to find their information elsewhere. When designing your webpages or thinking up titles for articles and ebooks, you should give the headline just as much consideration as the rest of your message—if not more.

In this chapter, I will go into the basic theory behind headline generation, including taking a look at why headlines are so powerful and the psychology of good copywriting. After we get the theory out of the way, I will introduce you to a fail-proof system that can generate great headlines to work as a jumping-off point to get your creative juices flowing. By understanding the elements of great copywriting and manipulating them to create the message you want, you can ensure the greatest chances for success.

Why Headlines Work

Creating a headline is not the same as writing a title for a book report in elementary school or an article in a peer-reviewed science journal. The point of those titles is to accurately describe or summarize the message of the report. They might be accurate, but they are not very interesting to people who do not already have a vested interest in the subject.

A catchy headline serves just one purpose: It grabs a reader's attention and encourages him or her to keep reading. In order to do this, you will need to tap into the reader's psychology. Fortunately, people have similar psychological hard-wiring, so a handful of common copywriting tactics will be effective for much of your audience.

In general, the most effective headlines are those that hint at solutions to problems that a reader is facing. The goal of a good headline is to make the reader sit up straight and say, "I need to know this!" By immediately answering the "What's in it for me?" question, your headline proves its relevancy to the reader's needs and incites further action.

> *In general, the most effective headlines are those that hint at solutions to problems that a reader is facing.*

There are a few tried-and-true methods for tapping into a reader's needs to pique his curiosity:

- Reveal a secret. People want fresh, new information, not a rehashing of things they've seen before. If readers think that you will deliver something fresh, they will be interested. Better yet, if they think they will learn something that few other people know, they will be especially eager to read more.

- Instill fear. Before you can offer a solution, you need to have a problem. Many people don't realize that they face a given problem until it's pointed out to them. If your headline suggests that a reader has been either misled or uninformed about a topic, and that this lack of information is dangerous, you will immediately capture their attention. For these headlines, your motto is, "What you don't know will hurt you."

- Promise pleasure. Aside from avoiding pain, all people are interested in seeking pleasure. These are the two most basic needs of human psychology. If your headline promises positive, appealing results that are quick or easy to obtain, you will capture the reader's interest.

- Ask a question. Readers are immediately more engaged with questions than basic statements. Why? Because questions demand answers. If your headline asks your readers a direct question, they will immediately be moved to answer it. If your headline asks why a certain thing happens in a particular way, your readers will immediately wonder, "Why is that?" and want to learn more.

- Offer social proof. Subconsciously, people want to feel that they are part of a community or that their opinions match up with those of others whom they respect. If a headline shows that billionaires, happy people, successful people, experts, or any other authoritative group endorses a particular product or feels a certain way, you will catch the attention of your readers.

As with any other piece of good copywriting, a headline introduces a problem and hints at a solution. When you craft your headline, you should always be thinking in terms of what the reader wants and how you can give it to them.

Once you know that, you will begin to see which methods are the most effective for capturing their attention.

Honesty Is Important

There is one danger in writing a headline, and that is the temptation to mislead your reader. A great headline might attract your visitors' attention and encourage them to read more, but if the content he sees does not fulfill the headline's promise, it will leave a bad taste in their mouth and ruin the trust you should be trying to build.

If you spend time online, you will quickly see how frustrated people become over "clickbait" headlines, or headlines designed just to get attention without offering anything valuable in response. This phenomenon has made many Web users cynical and leery of any overly enticing headline, making a copywriter's job harder than ever.

Remember that everything you do with a prospect is a value exchange. Your visitors are giving you their time in exchange for information. If your information is not as valuable as the time they spend reading it, they will understandably feel cheated. Their trust in you is broken, and they will not be likely to return.

Therefore, when crafting your headlines, it is imperative that you remain honest. Be enticing, but don't make a promise that you can't keep.

Anatomy of a Good Headline

As I explained above, good headlines will entice readers by introducing problems, asking questions, establishing the authority of others, and so on. The best headlines can do more than one of these things at a time. Think about some good headlines that you've come across in your own life. They likely did double duty by promising fresh information, surprising ideas, or desirable results about topics that are important to your life.

I am going to introduce you to a fail-proof system for creating headlines that work. Before I get there, though, I want to explain why the template works.

When you are writing a headline for an informative article, you can rely on the reader's curiosity or desire to learn more about a topic. If you are writing a more sales-focused message, however, your headline needs to focus more heavily on answering, "What's in it for me?" Remember, your readers are exchanging their time for your message; later, you will want them to exchange their money for your product or service. In order to build their trust and incite action, you will need to make it clear from the beginning that you are going to solve a problem.

Here's how you do this:

- First, you introduce the problem.
- Then, you suggest that you have a solution for this problem.

- Finally, you hint that your solution is easier, faster, or otherwise superior than any other solution.

You will see, time and again, that these principles are the foundation of all sales-related headlines. Although there are numerous variations, the core message is always similar. Recognizing this will help you understand why these templates are so effective and how to modify them to fit your needs.

A Few Additional Writing Tips

Before I describe my system and show you how to make it work for you, I have a few general writing tips that you can follow to make your headlines stand out:

- Study other headlines in your niche. You will want to know what your competition is saying so that you can say it better. This will also give you inspiration and ideas both for the headlines themselves and for your content.
- Whenever you talk about numerical results, such as how much money an activity has earned you, use an odd number instead of an even one. This is because, on a subconscious level, odd numbers seem more "real" or genuine. If you say that you earned $500.00 over the weekend, your claim will not be as believable as if you said you earned $497.23. Odd numbers seem more specific, since they have not been rounded off, and that specificity makes your claim seem more genuine.
- Figure out exactly what your prospect needs. Nothing communicates more directly to a prospect than

the headline. You should do enough market research that you can effectively write a headline that seems to read the prospect's mind. This means understanding the prospect's goals, hopes, and fears, and speaking to those directly.

> *You should do enough market research that you can effectively write a headline that seems to read the prospect's mind.*

- Be prepared to write several drafts. Using my templates will cut down a lot of your brainstorming time, but you will still need to tweak the results to achieve the perfect finished product. Your headline is important; so don't be worried if it takes more time to get it right than it took to write the content that accompanies it.

Now that I have gone over the basics, let's get into the details of my foolproof headline generation system!

Creating Headlines That Sell

Up until this point, I have been addressing the theory behind writing great headlines, and this is the place where most books will stop. Instead of giving you some tips and turning you loose to figure out the rest on your own, I would like to introduce you to a simple but effective system for generating great headlines.

When you were a kid, did you ever play with "Mad Libs"?

You can use the same general idea to create headlines.

36 Templates You Can Use Today

In this section, I will offer some basic headline templates and discuss why they are effective. In the next section, I will go into the variables in great detail. For now, just pay attention to the structure of the headline so you can see how it works. I will list the template first, followed by a couple of examples, and then analyze the results.

1 [Incredibly Good] without [Incredibly Bad]

"Free Traffic without Link Building"
"Lose Weight without Counting Calories"

This headline relies on your knowledge of your readers. You need to identify both what they want and what is standing in their way. Once you have that information, you just need to offer your readers what they want while removing a barrier that held them back in the past.

2 How [Premise] Got Me [Awesome Outcome]

"How Natural Link Building Got Me Natural, Relevant and Authoritative Links"
"How Taking Online Surveys Got Me a New Plasma TV"

This template works best when your prospect is inclined to be skeptical about your premise. By combining the premise with a personal testimony about great results, you offer an endorsement that will soften the prospect's doubts.

3 Are You [in This Kind of Pain or Anxiety]? Are You Sure?

"Are You Unable to Get Quality, Relevant, Authoritative Links to Your Blog? Are You Sure?"
"Are You Unable to Stick to Your Diet During the Holidays? Are You Sure?"

This sneaky headline works by casting doubt on a prospect's assumptions. You start by raising a question that strikes right at the heart of your readers' concerns. Then, by asking them to rethink their position, you subtly suggest that there is an alternative your readers hadn't thought of before. This sets the stage for you to offer an innovative solution in the content of your site or article.

4 How I [Achieved an Awesome Outcome][Overcoming a Massive Disadvantage]

"How I Increased Organic Traffic by 1,000% without a Link Building, AdWords, or Facebook Ads Budget"
"How I Lost 100 Pounds without Limiting My Favorite Foods"

As in our first example, this headline works by identifying a prospect's problem and barriers to solving that problem. In this case, you have boosted your credibility by offering a personal endorsement as well: The headline is reporting your experience, not a hypothetical situation. This works well when the outcome you're claiming may be harder for a prospect to take at face value.

5 How to [Live the Promise/Have the Result We Provide] by [A Low Magnitude Change, Activity or Situation]

"How to Have Incredible Organic Traffic by Joining Like-Minded Individuals to Deliver and Receive Authoritative Links"

"How to Become Debt Free by Making Just One Change to Your Monthly Budget"

The value of this headline is that it suggests to the readers that their goals are easily within their grasp. By highlighting a simple, easy change or activity, you convince your readers that achieving their goals is easier than they imagined. This will urge them to read the rest to see how to put this simple change to work.

6 For the [Prospect in Pain/Problem We Solve], How to [Live the Promise/Have the Result We Provide] Starting with [a Low Magnitude Change, Activity or Situation]

"For a Site with No Organic Traffic: How to Have Incredible Organic Traffic by Joining Like-Minded Individuals to Deliver and Receive Authoritative Links"

"For People in Debt: How to Live Debt-Free by Making
Just One Change to Your Monthly Budget"

This is a variation on the headline above. You will see that
the basic format is the same, but you have added one important element: You have identified your prospect by
name. This drives the message home that the person you
are targeting really is the person in the best position to act
on the plan you're about to explain.

7 If You Can [Easy Way to Start], Then You Can Have [Awesome Outcome]

"If You Can Paste Your Blog Articles into a Form, Then
You Can Have Natural, Relevant, Authoritative Links"
"If You Can Exercise Just 10 Minutes a Day, Then You
Can Lose 100 Pounds in a Year"

The hardest part of achieving any goal is getting started. If
you can convince your readers that overcoming inertia and
taking the first step is all they need to get on the path to
success, you will quickly incite them to action.

8 Secrets/Tricks/Strategies/Techniques/Systems of a [Prospect Who Is Living the Promise]

"Secrets of a Site with Significant Traffic from Non-Paid
Sources"
"Secrets of a Young Millionaire"

This headline uses subtle social pressure to help win over your prospect. You identify a person or group that the prospect would admire or wish to become, and then offer to divulge a secret or strategy that the successful person employs. This works well because the reader will immediately wonder, "What do they know that I don't?" and will read on to find out.

9 Warning/Alert/Attention/Be Advised—[Type of Prospect] Will [Situation More Painful Than the Pain]

"Be Advised: Bloggers Will Receive a Google Penalty for Spammy Link-Building Practices"

"Warning: Dieters Who Cut Too Many Calories Will Gain Even More Weight"

As I explained above, a person's primary motive will always be to avoid pain and maximize pleasure or good results. This headline takes full advantage of that knowledge by introducing a surprising source of pain. It works by taking something a prospect might already be doing or considering and showing why it is actually the wrong choice. The reader will want to know the better solution.

10 Show Me [Prospect in Pain/Problem We Solve] and I Will Show You How to Have [Awesome Outcome]

"Show Me a Site with No Organic Traffic, and I Will Show You How to Have a Site with Significant Traffic from Non-Paid Sources"

"Show Me a Person Living with Debt, and I Will Show You How to Have a Debt-Free Life within One Year"

This type of headline is designed to drive home your authority and knowledge on a particular topic. It works well because your prospect will identify with the first half and want to see what solution you can offer that will provide the second half. The more enticing the second half sounds, the better the odds that a reader will stick around to see it.

11 [Number of Statistics] of a [Type of Prospect] Are [Now Living the Promised Land] Despite [Initial Negative Reaction to the Premise]

"50 Percent of Bloggers are Growing Traffic with Authoritative Linking Despite Not Having a Dedicated Link Builder"

"50 Percent of Dieters Are Losing Weight Despite Not Going to the Gym"

This type of headline works well to invert a reader's expectations. You will want to identify something that is part of the "prevailing wisdom" on a topic or an assumption that your readers might have. Then, you will show that a surprising number of people are seeing success without doing whatever the reader assumes is necessary. By simplifying the process, you will pique your readers' interest.

12 NUMBER of ways to [Reach the Shore of the Promised Land] [without Increasing Pain/Effort/ Anxiety/Loss]

"10 Ways to Have Incredible Organic Traffic without Working Countless Hours Contacting Webmasters for Links"

"Five Ways to Live a Debt-Free Life without Giving Up Your Favorite Activities"

People are always looking for a way to "have it all," and this headline makes the promise that it's possible. By identifying what your prospects might be afraid of losing, you can assure them that it is still possible to reach their goals without sacrificing that important element.

13 The Mistake People Make with [Incredibly Good]

"The Mistake People Make with Free Traffic"

"The Mistake People Make with Losing 100 Pounds in a Year"

This is another headline that works by inverting your readers' expectations. It targets prospects who think they already understand the topic; then it throws a curve ball at them by introducing a mistake they might not know about. This will encourage them to look at your solution rather than rely on their own knowledge.

14 The Mistake People Make with [Incredibly Bad]

"The Mistake People Make with Link Building"

"The Mistake People Make with Counting Calories"

This works in the opposite way of the headline above. This headline works best when it's targeting a reader who may not realize the negative consequences of some actions, especially if those actions are part of the prevailing wisdom on a topic.

15 This Mistake Cost Me [Average Cost of Doing It the Hard Way]

"This Mistake Cost Me $1793.23"

If there is one thing most readers can agree on, it's that losing money is always a bad thing. By showing how your readers are wasting their money by doing something in a certain way, you can convert them to a different method. Remember to use an odd number for your example to boost your credibility!

16 Ends Tonight (Save [Average Cost of Doing It the Hard Way]) "Ends Tonight (Save $1793.23)"

This headline borrows its key component from an age-old sales tactic. By taking the above premise and adding a time limit, you instill a sense of urgency in your readers. Not only must they take action to prevent wasting money, they must act right away or miss out on the opportunity.

17 Why You May Never [Live the Promise/Have the Result We Provide]

"Why You May Never Have Incredible Organic Traffic"
"Why You May Never Have a Debt-Free Life"

This type of headline utilizes reverse psychology. When you tell your readers that they may never achieve their goal, you elicit an indignant response. They will want to know why you think they won't succeed, and this will compel them to read on. It also suggests that you know the right answer or solution to help them.

18 Do You Still Want to [Live the Promise/Have the Result We Provide]?

"Do You Still Want to Have Incredible Organic Traffic?"
"Do You Still Want to Live Debt-Free?"

This is another headline designed to elicit an indignant response. Faced with this question, your readers are likely to answer, "Of course I do!" However, simply by asking the question, you have planted a seed of doubt in your readers' minds, and they will read on to see whether you know something that they don't.

19 I Am Looking for [Type of Prospect]

"I Am Looking for Bloggers!"

This headline takes a different approach. Rather than making a promise to your readers, it reaches out directly to your target audience. Because you are asking for them by name, your readers will feel an immediate link to you. They will wonder why you are looking for them specifically and be more receptive to taking direct action.

20 Ridiculously Simple [Awesome Outcome]

"Ridiculously Simple, Natural, Relevant, Authoritative Links"

"Ridiculously Simple Breakfast Foods That Melt Off the Pounds"

Time and again, we have seen that your prospects are looking for the simplest, easiest solutions to their problems. By labeling your outcome as "ridiculously simple," you imply that it's so easy there is no way your readers could possibly fail.

21 For [Type of Prospect] Only

"For Bloggers Only"

This is a variation on number 19. Again, you are speaking directly to the audience that you're targeting, but this time you are creating an air of exclusivity. This headline suggests subconsciously that your prospects are eligible to receive some type of knowledge that is classified or otherwise unavailable to the population at large, and that sort of exclusivity can really pique curiosity.

22 NUMBER Proven Ways to [Reach the Shore of the Promised Land]

"Five Proven Ways to Have Incredible Organic Traffic"

"Seven Proven Ways to Lose 100 Pounds in One Year"

This headline is simple but effective. It combines an enticing opportunity with a concrete number of "proven" steps. People are more likely to believe a claim that is backed up by evidence, and saying in the headline that you have that evidence is a great way to win over some skeptics.

23 NUMBER Reasons Why You Should Join [Product Offering]

"Seven Reasons Why You Should Join LinkMatchmaker. com"

This headline is for when you are actively pushing a prospect to buy a particular product or service. It is straightforward and honest, and it works best if your prospects are already familiar with your product. Anyone who finds this headline is likely to be receptive to or even asking for a sales pitch, so this is the prime opportunity to really woo your prospects.

24 If You Change THIS, You Will [Reach the Shore of the Promised Land]

"If You Change THIS, You Will Have Incredible Organic Traffic"

"If You Change THIS, You Will Have a Debt-Free Life"

This headline works for two reasons. First, it suggests that your readers are very close to solving their problems; they are just one simple change away from being able to realize their goals. Second, it's built around a mystery. Your readers will be itching to know what "THIS" refers to, and their curiosity will convert to a click.

25 [Incredibly Good], [Awesome Outcome] and [Incredibly Bad]

"Free Traffic, Natural, Relevant, Authoritative Links and Link Building"

"Losing Weight, Feeling Amazing, and Counting Calories"

This headline relies on the dissonance formed between the first two positive attributes and the final negative one. The reader should pause and think, "Wait, one of these doesn't fit." The effect is strongest when the third item is especially negative, as this will incite the most curiosity about how it all fits together.

26 [Incredibly Bad] Sucks!

"Link Building Sucks!"

Short, to the point, and brutally honest, this headline relies on shock value to catch a reader's attention. Most readers are not anticipating such frank language, but you would be surprised how often this exact phrase gets typed into search engines by people looking for strong opinions on a topic.

27 [Product Offering] Is a No Brainer. Here's Why...

"Link Matchmaker Is a No Brainer. Here's Why..."

This is another product-oriented headline for a sales message. This one makes it clear that you are about to launch into a sales pitch, but if your product is familiar to your prospects, your explanation will be welcome. Since you have made it clear from the headline that you'll be explaining why your product is superior, readers go in knowing exactly what to expect.

28 Get Rid of [Incredibly Bad] Once and for All

"Get Rid of Link Building Once and for All!"
"Get Rid of Debt Once and for All!"

Some problems crop up repeatedly throughout a prospect's life. If you have a permanent solution, this headline will convert many excited prospects who just want someone to fix their problem. This headline sends the message that you have the final word on a topic, which immediately builds your authority.

29 Who Else Wants to [Deliver You to the Promised Land]?

"Who Else Wants to Receive Traffic Directly From Google?"

"Who Else Wants to Lose 100 Pounds in a Year?"

This format relies on social cues to subtly nudge your prospect toward engaging with your message. By using the term "Who else," you suggest that others have already achieved whatever the prospect wants. Your readers, then, may fear that they're falling behind and will be eager to get the help they need to catch up.

30 Thousands Now [Deliver You to the Promised Land] Who Never Thought They Could

"Thousands Now Receive Traffic Directly from Google Who Never Thought They Could"

"Thousands Now Enjoy a Debt-Free Lifestyle Who Never Thought They Could"

This headline appeals to the inner pessimist in your prospect. By appealing directly to a visitor's doubts, you make it clear that you understand their hesitation but know that they can overcome their problem. Combined with the social pressure that "thousands" of others have already succeeded, this message can be very powerful.

31 Create/Build/Get Own/Have (a) [Incredibly Good] You Can Be Proud Of

"Have Free Traffic You Can Be Proud Of"

"Have a Body You Can Be Proud Of"

This headline works by identifying your readers end goal

and making them personally invested in it. Most people want to feel proud of their accomplishments, and suggesting that you can help a person achieve that feeling will pique your readers' interest.

32 Give Me [Surprisingly Short Period of Time for Results] and I'll Give You [Incredibly Good]

"Give Me 48 Days, and I'll Give You Free Traffic"
"Give Me 30 Days, and I'll Give You a Debt-Free Life"

People love instant gratification. By suggesting that a positive result could be obtained in a shorter period than the reader expects, you will gain his or her attention. Coupling this with your own authority further builds trust and boosts curiosity.

33 The Lazy [Type of Prospect] Way/Guide to [Incredibly Good]

"The Lazy Blogger's Way to Free Traffic"
"A Lazy Girl's Guide to a Flat Tummy"

Readers want to maximize their results and minimize the effort it takes to achieve them. It's little wonder that "lazy" guides have such broad appeal. This type of headline seems to make the claim that anyone can achieve the desired results quickly, easily, or without much effort.

34 Do You Make These [Incredibly Bad] Mistakes?

"Do You Make These Link Building Mistakes?"
"Do You Make These Calorie Counting Mistakes?"

This headline piques readers' curiosity and also acts to incite fear. Readers may not have realized that their actions were a mistake until this point, but they will be eager to find out whether they're doing things correctly once they see this headline.

35 [Live the Promise/Have the Result We Provide] Like [an Expert in This Field]

"Have Incredible Organic Traffic Like an SEO Guru"
"Have a Debt-Free Life Like a Financial Expert"

This headline, like many others, works by identifying a group that your prospects admire and suggesting that they can be just like them. It's human nature to want to fit in with people you respect, and calling on the experts in any given field lends credibility to your claim: After all, if an expert can do it, a novice should be able to learn.

36 If You Don't Get [Incredibly Good], You'll Hate Yourself Later

"If You Don't Get Free Traffic, You'll Hate Yourself Later"

"If You Don't Become Debt-Free This Year, You'll Hate Yourself Later"

This headline makes use of a not-so-subtle threat to drive the message home. By making it clear that inaction has unpleasant consequences, you incite readers to act. This creates a sense of panic that will encourage prospects to read your message for a solution to the problem you pose.

Variables

You probably noticed as you browsed the above headlines that certain words and phrases came up repeatedly. These are the variables that are plugged into the templates, and they will vary depending on what you are writing. In fact, the templates are so versatile that they will support any type of variable: As long as the item you fit inside the bracket matches the variable description, the resulting headline will make good sense.

Here's a closer look at those variables and what exactly you should use for each one:

1 Incredibly Good

This is the carrot that you're putting out to attract your prospects. The "Incredibly Good" is the positive result that your reader craves and that can be achieved by applying your method or using your product.

2 Incredibly Bad

The "Incredibly Bad" could be any negative consequence, but it's most effective if it's tied to the "old" or traditional way of doing something. The "Incredibly Bad" is what you are avoiding by using your product or service.

3 Premise

The premise is your core argument, or the basic idea of what you are trying to sell. For example, if you're selling a diet pill, your premise might be "rapid weight loss." If you're selling a pest control service, your premise could be a "pest-free home."

4 Awesome Outcome

This is more than the "Incredibly Good" you describe above. Your "Awesome Outcome" is the best possible result of using your product or service. It's the best goal your prospect might be reaching for.

5 Prospect in Pain/Problem We Solve

Prospects come to you because they have a problem. If you can identify that problem or point to the cause of their pain, they will be more eager to believe that you can solve it through your product or service.

6 Overcoming a Massive Disadvantage

People want to know that it is possible to succeed even when it seems difficult. This variable basically applies to the roadblock that's standing between the reader and his or her goals.

7 A Low Magnitude Change, Activity, or Situation

If your system seems too difficult, a reader will not be interested. You need to introduce changes slowly and carefully. A great example of the low magnitude change is the phrase, "For the price of a cup of coffee..." The idea of solving world hunger is overwhelming, but paying a few dollars at a time is much more manageable.

8 Living the Promise

This refers to any situation where someone is already living the kind of results you intend to deliver through your product or service. A person who has achieved whatever the prospect wants is one who's living the promise.

9 Type of Prospect

Wherever you see this in the template, it's a signal to input the name for your target audience. You can make this as vague or as specific as you want, and it might be beneficial to try several versions to see which is the most effective at reaching your intended readers.

10 Not Increasing Pain/Effort/Anxiety/Loss

Your prospects want to make their lives easier and avoid complications. This is a variable that speaks to that concern directly. Use a phrase like "Without going into debt" or "Without feeling deprived" in this space.

Putting It All Together

Now that you have seen some useful templates and an explanation of the variables, you can start plugging in your own terms to generate headlines about nearly anything. By changing out the variables, you can keep using the same templates for a variety of subjects, and save yourself a lot of work.

Of course, the end result will still require some tweaking. Once you have landed on a template that works well for your goals, you will probably want to modify the phrasing a little to make things flow smoothly. The finished product should make good grammatical sense and flow easily when read aloud to prevent confusing your readers.

> *Keep a list of your finished headlines as you write them so that you can refer to them later and pick the most effective one.*

Keep a list of your finished headlines as you write them so that you can refer to them later and pick the most effective one. You might even want to release the same report in a few different channels with a few different headlines to test which one is the most effective.

Automating Your Headline Creation

Although you can manually fill out your headline templates like a traditional Mad Lib, I do have a tool that can make your life a lot easier. Visit http://ContentFirst.Marketing/HeadlineTool for my headline generator, which automatically generates headlines based on the variables that you input. It includes all the templates discussed in this guide, plus many more; and results can be fully customized with your unique variables to ensure that no two headlines will be exactly the same.

Putting Your Headlines to Work

Your headline is vitally important to attracting readers and converting visitors into prospects, but a good headline is not enough to sell a product. You will need to back up your claims with solid writing and, of course, an exemplary product.

Fortunately, the core ideas behind great headlines also apply to the rest of your content. Copywriting hangs on your ability to introduce a problem, create a crisis and offer a solution. If you can achieve those three things, you can create a compelling sales message that will win over your prospects and convert them to customers.

4 GET MORE TRAFFIC WITH LINK BUILDING

T he task of search engine optimization, or boosting your webpage's rank in search engine results, is vital to the success of your website. No matter how valuable your site's content, you will not get traffic if it doesn't appear high on the list of search results for its niche.

SEO has changed dramatically over the years, responding in large part to changes made to the search engines themselves. As searching technology improves and becomes more sophisticated, the path to the first page of search engine results changes. Many old SEO tactics no longer work, and some things that didn't even exist a decade ago are now of utmost importance to page ranking.

> *No matter how valuable your site's content, you will not get traffic if it doesn't appear high on the list of search results for its niche.*

To help you navigate these changes, I will examine the current state of SEO in this chapter and provide you with practical tips for acquiring backlinks and boosting your site's visibility. Most importantly, these tips have been identified by SEO experts as having sticking power. By employing these strategies, you can ensure the value of your site in the long term, weathering the storms of Google algorithm changes without suffering a loss in page rank.

What Is a Backlink, Anyway?

A backlink, simply put, is a link placed on one page that leads back to a specific website. These links help to draw new visitors to the site in two ways. First, any visitor who finds a link and clicks it will be taken to the site. This directly boosts the site's traffic. Second, backlinks act as "votes" or endorsements in the eyes of search engines. Linked sites are viewed as being more authoritative and valuable. This means that sites with backlinks will rank more highly in search engine results than sites without backlinks.

In fact, acquiring the right kind of links is one of the most important parts of search engine optimization, as there is nothing that will boost your site's rank as quickly as a smart backlinking strategy. A poor backlinking strategy, however, will greatly harm your site. This is why it is so important to understand the principles of SEO before crafting any links to your site.

Recent Developments in SEO

For a long time, search engines found and indexed pages based upon the prevalence of certain keywords. Those keywords would appear within the page's content itself, as well as on other sites, with the keyword phrase linking back to the original site. This was the earliest function of backlinking, and it worked very well for many years.

In fact, the system worked too well, making it easy to exploit. A website could choose a few keywords that were linked to valuable AdSense ads, slap together some content around those words, and utilize software to generate hundreds or thousands of backlinks to that original page. Each link to the site would act as a vote, telling the search engines that the site was the best match for that keyword, and, at the time, the quantity of those links mattered much more than quality. In fact, the sites with the backlinks in them were never designed to be read by humans; they existed solely to be found by search engine spiders.

The keyword-added page would rise in the search engine ranks, gaining lots of clicks, and garnering plenty of income for the developer. This was good news for some developers, but it wasn't good for users: Finding real, valuable information about a topic became increasingly difficult as the Web filled with these shallow sites.

To penalize these sites and allow truly valuable content to rank highly, Google set to work rebuilding the way their searches worked. The search algorithm has been refined over several updates since 2011, including Panda, Penguin, and, most recently, Hummingbird. Each update brought something new to the table, but the underlying message was the same: Google would no longer tolerate sites with poor quality content, and it would reward sites with authority.

Black Hat, White Hat

If you spend any time at all learning about SEO practices, you will encounter the terms "black hat" and "white hat." These are the names for two distinct schools of thought in regards to website design.

White hat practices are those that conform to Google's recommendations and best practices. Essentially, white hat SEO follows the rules and uses technology as it was designed. These methods are legitimate and respectable, but they can take a lot of time and effort.

Black hat SEO, meanwhile, is based upon shortcuts and tricks. It could be considered a form of cheating. Black hat SEO exploits Google algorithms, using them in ways that were not intended. This can create immediate and dramatic short-term results.

The problem with black hat practices is that, while they may be good for the site developer, they are bad for consumers. Black hat tactics are the primary reason why Google has cracked down on poor website quality and backlinking strategies. It is not unreasonable to assume that Google and other search engines will continue to identify and penalize black hat strategies in the future.

For this reason, we recommend avoiding black hat tactics altogether. White hat SEO is mostly timeless: If you are acting in good faith to provide the highest quality product that you can, you will be rewarded. Sites that practice white hat tactics have traditionally suffered less from Google algorithm changes, and this trend will continue to be true for the foreseeable future. With that in mind, all the tactics discussed after this are in keeping with Google's best practices.

Authority: The New Standard of Quality

Before you begin trying to boost your visibility by using backlinks, you need to stop and ask yourself why your website deserves to rank highly in a Google search. Does your site offer something of value that no one else is offering? If the answer to that is "No," then no amount of backlinking will help your site grow. Today's Google algorithms demand high-quality content, and this includes originality, quality writing and useful information.

Google determines whether a site has authority in several ways. In general, it strives to give the highest page rank to content that is authoritative. This strategy makes sense from a user perspective. After all, if you were searching for the health benefits of juicing, wouldn't you rather get your information from a site written by a nutritionist than an anonymous page? Google certainly thinks so, and that's why expert sites rank the highest in search results.

Several factors go into building a page's authority:

- The vocabulary used on a site. This goes beyond simple keyword phrases. Instead, it involves the use of certain niche vocabulary that is used naturally by an expert writing within a certain field. These niche words and phrases are what Google currently uses to identify content about a given topic. Because the topic of a site is determined by the presence of these phrases, you may find sites in your Google results that are relevant to your search without including any of the words you actually searched for. This is because the goal of modern search engines is to respond to a user's intention, not his exact search string.

- Whether authoritative sites link back to that site as a reference. When a high-quality, well-respected site links to another website, it is a clear vote that the other site is valuable as well. This is the key for developing quality backlinks in today's SEO environment. The quality of the site that links to your page is just as important as the quality of your page itself.

The Internet used to be anonymous. Today, social media has largely removed anonymity from the Web. If you want your site to succeed, you will need to use your web presence to build a trusted, authoritative brand. That brand will be crucial for building backlinks, boosting your search engine results and encouraging reader trust in your site.

> *If you want your site to succeed, you will need to use your web presence to build a trusted, authoritative brand.*

Where Have All the Websites Gone?

As authoritative websites with rich content rise to the top of search results, many once-popular sites have dropped from view entirely. This is not just because they have been out-competed by other sites: These shallow websites have actually been penalized by Google to keep them out of the top search results. In effect, sites that are over-optimized suffer from the effects of negative SEO.

If your website has recently suffered a severe drop in page rank, it may be due to Google penalties. These penalties might be due to the content of your page itself, but they could also be caused by the backlinks leading to your page. If poor-quality sites all link back to a certain page, that page will suffer a loss of rank.

This means that a site that was perfectly optimized a few years ago might now be practically invisible. Even worse, many so-called SEO experts are still encouraging old methods, such as automated backlink generation and spun article content, so you could end up paying for help only to see your rank drop instead of rise.

A Note on Negative SEO

Google insists that there is no such thing as negative SEO. Most likely, it says this in an attempt to dissuade black hat SEO practitioners from de-ranking their competitors. In theory, it should be possible to cause another person's website to lose rank by creating thousands of spammy backlinks. These low-quality backlinks would penalize the site they linked to, ultimately causing it to lose its position in the SERP.

In practice, this is probably not something worth trying. Not only is it dishonest, it's also likely to backfire: If the activity is linked back to you, you will surely suffer penalties of your own, and they may be more severe than a loss of page rank.

If you feel that you have been the victim of negative SEO or just want to have your site's link removed from spammy listings, you do have one recourse. Using Google's "Disavow" tool, you can report low-quality links in hopes that they will be taken down. Note that reporting a site does not guarantee that Google will take action. You may want to start by approaching the other site owner first to request the link be taken down. Only if he refuses this request should you try the Disavow tool.

The Anatomy of a Great Backlink

While the concept behind backlinking is the same as it has always been, the practice of actually creating these links is a little bit different. In general, the current trend in SEO leans heavily toward authoritative sites written by experts, and backlinking practices reflect this.

A few years ago, a good backlink existed inside the text. Generally, the keyword in a text was linked back to the site that was built around the keyword. When a visitor reviewed the page, he or she could click the linked word to be taken to a site that would ostensibly provide more information about that keyword.

Today, this type of keyword-based linking is no longer preferred. The reason is largely because such links can appear spammy after several years of over-use. Readers are often reluctant to click on these embedded links because they are not sure where the link is heading and don't know whether it's safe and informative.

Instead of using keyword-based backlinks, focus instead on using links that are more academic in nature. You can build your links in many ways:

- Link to a website by using its title or bare URL within the text of the article.
- Use an obvious linking phrase such as "find more information about <your product> here."
- Make a list of sources at the end of an article. Use foot-

notes if necessary. This lends a page a sense of authority by mirroring academic citations.

- Reserve your backlink for your author biography at the end of an article rather than stuffing it inside the article itself.

The value of these links is that they make it clear to the reader what he or she is about to click on and why it's valuable. In today's virtual landscape, gaining the trust of visitors is your most important job as a website creator.

Building Backlinks Safely and Naturally

Now that we have looked at the way Google's search algorithms have changed and seen what type of content is rewarded, you may be wondering how you can safely build your page's search rank. If you have lost rank due to over-optimization or are starting anew, you will want to focus on creating excellent content and building high-quality backlinks.

Create Content Users Will Share for You

The easiest way to build backlinks is to encourage others to do it for you. Natural links are the single most valuable method of boosting page rank. They are also the most elusive. In order to get natural links, you will need to create valuable content that people will naturally want to share with their friends and family. Strive to create content that people will want to save, reference, or pass along.

Social media is one of the most important aspects of the Internet today, and you should always have social media in mind when designing your website. Think of ways to make it easier for people to share your content. Here are some particularly share-worthy types of content that you can use to generate natural backlinks:

- Images, such as infographics and memes, are highly shareable due to the visual nature of social media.
- Quizzes that prompt the user to share their results are popular in social media as well and can provide information and generate activity on your page.
- Tools and resources, such as currency converters, recipe calculators and more, get shared frequently because they are so useful.
- Recipes, instructions, and other types of genuinely useful content are more likely to be shared than something more abstract that cannot be put into action.

When generating content for your website, think about what you personally enjoy on the Internet. Pay attention to what is shared on social media among friends and family, especially people in the target audience for your site's niche. Find ways to create and deliver that

> *When generating content for your website, think about what you personally enjoy on the Internet.*

type of content on a regular basis.

Additionally, make backlinking easy. The more effort someone has to put into sharing your content, the less likely they will be to do it. When you post an infographic on your site, include a code that can be easily copied and pasted by another website owner or blogger. This allows a visitor to share that content and its embedded link with minimal effort. Also be sure that every page of your site or post on your blog has unobtrusive but visible buttons to share the content to Facebook, Pinterest, Twitter, LinkedIn, and other social media sites.

When you create content that is easy to share, many of your backlinks will develop organically. This saves you the trouble of building up backlinks yourself, and it builds traffic and visitor involvement. Having readers share your content is the holy grail of SEO, and it should be encouraged as much as possible.

Traditional Sources of Backlinks That Still Work

While having your readers build backlinks for you is the ultimate goal, it is not something that you can rely on. This is especially true when your site is new and finding its audience. No one can share your content if your page is hidden deep in Google's search results!

Although the rules of SEO have changed somewhat in the last few years, many old backlinking strategies can and will still work if you are careful about applying them:

- Article marketing. Instead of posting spun articles on dozens of free sites, focus on posting one high-quality, informative article on a popular, well-respected website in your niche. Place your link in your author biography or, where relevant, reference your own blog posts by their title rather than using keywords as anchor text.
- Guest posting. This is similar to article marketing, but it uses blogs rather than article sites. Essentially, you will create a blog post for another blogger to publish. That post will contain a link back to your website, whether within the blog's text or as part of your biography. For best results, find a popular, well-traveled blog in your niche. Aside from providing a valuable backlink, guest posting can help get your work in front of a fresh audience, and you may gain blog subscribers this way.
- Forum posts. Use forums within your niche to build up your personal authority on a subject rather than spamming your link. People will come to see you as a helpful, knowledgeable person and will seek out your website for more information. Keep a link in your forum profile or signature space.
- eBook publishing. Self-publishing an ebook is a relatively new but valuable method for building your audience and generating links back to your site. The book does not need to be very long, especially if you're

offering it for free. Take the time to create valuable content worthy of sharing, and then post the book to a site like Scribed that will allow you to upload PDF files. You can also self-publish an ebook to Amazon or Smashwords. This allows you to link to your site from the book itself as well as your author profile.

- Video sites. YouTube, Vimeo, and other sites that allow users to create and post their own videos can be valuable for gaining visitors and building links. Keep the video short, entertaining, and useful. The more value the video gives to viewers, the more likely they will be to share it. Add your backlink to the video's description and your profile page.

- Question sites. Places like Yahoo Answers and Quora serve a dual purpose. One, they function like forums in establishing you as an expert in your field. Two, they give you insight into what questions are being asked about a given topic, giving you inspiration for rich content for your site. Create accounts with links to your site in the profile, and use these accounts to answer questions related to your niche.

- Resource pages. Link directories are not as valuable as they once were, but they can still be effective backlinking tools if the directory rests on an authoritative website. Look for a site with a high page rank and lots of stellar content, and see if there's a "resources" page or similar link list that would match your site. For example, if your site sold aquarium supplies, you might look for fish enthusiast sites that list resources for people building their own tank setups.

Your goal is to use these backlinks to show that your own site is informative and authoritative. You want to establish your authority in your niche and build trust with readers. Make this your primary objective as you seek out backlinking opportunities. The page rank boost of having your link scattered across the Internet is a secondary benefit that will come naturally as you build your brand.

If the idea of posting valuable, original articles on high-authority websites seems daunting, don't worry: You will not need more than a few of these articles to reap the rewards. Today's SEO values quality over quantity, so a careful strategy will be much more effective than a shotgun approach.

A Few Backlink Opportunities for Your Business

The ideas discussed above will provide you with plenty of rich opportunities for building backlinks and generating traffic back to your website. By and large, however, they work best with content-heavy websites that deal primarily in information. If you are running a business, your website is important, but you may not have much content left over to publish to other websites.

In this case, article marketing and related tactics will not work as well for you. Fortunately, business websites have other opportunities at their disposal that can generate rich backlinks of their own:

- List your business with a link to its website on every listing and review page that you can, such as Yelp or YellowPages.com. Not only will this create links back to your site, it will help you gather feedback from customers and boost your overall web presence.

- If your company is always looking for new talent, online job listing sites can provide an excellent link back to your site while getting your job opening in front of qualified candidates. These listings are frequently shared among friends or families as well, boosting your numbers.

- If you run a business, check local sites for your community. Some cities have calendars of upcoming events, and you may have a relevant event to list there, such as a customer appreciation day, half-price day, or similar deal.

- If you offer any coupons or special deals, list your website on deal sites, particularly those targeted to your specific geographic location.

- If you have partners, affiliates or vendors, see if you can have your page listed on their sites. Vendors are often happy to list their clients on their website as a way to show how successful the business is. If your business provides a service, ask to have a testimonial with a backlink placed on your client's website.

These are just a few ideas to get you started. As you develop your company's marketing plan, you may come up with many more. In general, anything you can do to raise awareness about your company can also create a backlink, boosting your site's rank and improving your Web presence.

Beyond Backlinking: Other Strategies for Boosting Page Rank

Backlinking is important, but it is not the only thing you can do to improve your search engine ranking. In fact, if you are looking to boost your presence in search engine results, there are two other things you should be doing: You should be using internal links, and you should boost the value of your backlinks.

Internal Linking

If a backlink is a link back to your page from another website, an internal link connects two pages within your website together. In general, search engines will view sites with extensive linking favorably. Think of a site like Wikipedia, where all the content is linked together to provide

> *If a backlink is a link back to your page from another website, an internal link connects two pages within your website together.*

deeper meaning, or an entertainment site like Cracked.com where one article leads seamlessly to the next. Internal links signal to the search engine that your content is rich, and rich, deep content is currently rewarded by high page ranks.

With that in mind, you do not want to overdo it. Too many links will start to appear spammy and will stop boosting the value of your page. In fact, the presence of apparently spammy links can actually cause your page to lose its rank. Therefore, use your internal links judiciously: Avoid stuffing them in where they don't belong.

One difference between internal and external links that you can use to your advantage is the use of keywords. For example, imagine that you run a website that sells shoes. On this site, you might have a page describing women's shoes. When you mention women's dress shoes, you would naturally discuss high heels, and linking "high heels" to your page about that type of shoe makes perfectly good sense.

Boosting Your Backlinks

If gaining backlinks for your own site can boost its authority and page rank, it stands to reason that links to the backlinking site would boost that site's authority as well. In fact, that is precisely what happens.

By building links back to the sites that backlink you, you boost their authority. This in turn improves the quality of your backlinks, driving up your organic search engine ranking. While it may seem counterproductive to publicize other sites in your niche, doing so ultimately rewards you.

The easiest way to boost your backlinks is to spread them on social media. You can make this do double duty by sharing the post or webpage where your link resides. This will publicize the content to readers who may not have already seen it, and it generates a fresh link on the Web to help boost the site's search engine ranking.

Another way to boost the value of your backlinking sites is to refer to them in your other articles. If the sites that have linked to you in the past are authoritative, valuable resources, you can use them as references in your article marketing, blog posts, and more. This can help boost the site's rank and create a trickle-down effect that will improve your own search engine ranking as well.

Looking Ahead to the Future of SEO

In this chapter I have focused on "white hat" SEO practices for growing website traffic and building page rank naturally. This is not just because white hat SEO is the more honest approach: It's also because it has the most longevity.

The reality is that no one can guarantee what the future holds for websites. As technology continues to evolve, search engines will modify their approach to meet the demands of increasingly savvy consumers. Today, social media reigns supreme. Tomorrow, it could be something totally new.

No matter what changes, however, the underlying principles of good SEO remain the same: High quality content that meets the needs and demands of its users will always rank more highly than anything else. By understanding how search engines work and striving to use the best practices laid out in their guidelines, you can stay on top of any changes and continue to enjoy good SEO.

Although it is impossible to say for certain what might happen in the future, it is safe to say that the most successful site owners will be those who are adaptable and willing to change their approach to keep their sites competitive. This is an ongoing process requiring research and attentiveness. SEO is not something you can do once and walk away; it's something that must be reviewed and refined over time to ensure that it is always generating the results you want.

My hope is that this chapter has given you the essentials you need to create excellent content and build a web of links that will boost its page authority and draw visitors to your site. From here, the rest is in your hands.

5 EMAIL ENGAGEMENT AND LANDING PAGE CREATION

If you have not yet established an email newsletter for your business, you are missing one of the most powerful marketing tools at your disposal. A successful email campaign boosts engagement with your audience and builds up the authority of your brand. It also acts as a bridge to link interested prospects with your products or services.

People who subscribe to your mailing list are already interested in your niche, making them the most valuable prospects for building your brand and delivering your message.

Simply stated, email marketing is the single best way to build a relationship with your customers. It is

> *Simply stated, email marketing is the single best way to build a relationship with your customers.*

an ongoing communication platform where you can share ideas and information directly with the people most interested in your message. All other marketing tactics, from social media interaction to paid advertisements, are of secondary importance. The way you interact with those who have already shown an investment in your brand will define the success of your endeavors.

Starting a mailing list is simple. All you need is a method for collecting email addresses and content to send to those subscribers. The details of building a successful campaign are a bit more complex, however, and in this chapter I will walk you through everything you need to know to get the most from your email newsletters.

Before You Build Your List

Before you can begin a successful email campaign, you will need to spend some time thinking about your goals. Emails can be used to sell a product or service; they can also serve as a way to boost your authority on a topic and build trust with your readers. First and foremost, however, your emails should be focused on helping your prospects with a specific problem that they face.

Think of it this way: Your prospects are interested in your product or service because it serves a need or solves a problem. No matter how clever your ideas or noble your cause, no one is going to give you business unless they get something in return. Looking at your newsletter from this "What's in it for me?" mentality will help you craft emails that will engage your readers and further your goals.

No matter how clever your ideas or noble your cause, no one is going to give you business unless they get something in return.

Every email that you craft needs to provide value to the reader. The usefulness of your emails determines the staying power of your list: If people start to feel bored or uninterested in your content, they will unsubscribe or simply ignore your emails. The key to gaining and keeping subscribers is to keep your focus permanently on servicing their needs in a way that also helps your business.

Deciding on a Niche

To identify what your readers want, you will first need to identify what niche your content will serve. Since your business already occupies a niche, this should prove as a valuable jumping-off point for developing a marketing strategy.

Think about what your target audience wants or needs. What issues do they encounter on a regular basis? What is holding them back from achieving what they want? How can you offer solutions to those problems? Asking these questions will help you build customized content that will drive business, build trust, and ensure that your subscribers remain satisfied.

You do not have to make these guesses in the dark. The easiest way to determine what your audience wants and needs is to go directly to the source. Find a place where your prospects are likely to spend time, such as a forum dedicated to your niche. Read their discussions to see what type of problems come up frequently or where people are looking for solutions. You can also see what types of questions are being asked about your niche on sites like Ask.com or Quora. This type of research will reveal not just the questions being asked but also the mindset behind those questions. This will help you spot the larger issues that can be addressed through your campaign.

Choosing the Right Campaign Type

Once you have identified the specific niche you will be servicing, it's time to start considering how you will tailor your approach to meet the needs of your subscribers. Before you can start creating content for your email marketing campaign, you will need to decide what type of campaign you'll be creating and what you hope to gain from it. The first step, choosing a niche, is focused on the needs of your readers. This step, choosing a campaign, is focused on your needs as a business owner.

Although there are plenty of nuances in how your campaign is run, as I will address later, all email-marketing campaigns ultimately fall into one of three categories:

- **Short-term revenue campaigns** are designed to convert quickly and directly to sales. Your message is just long enough to generate interest in your product before urging readers to act. These campaigns frequently take up just a few emails per product or service being sold, and they work quickly to pinpoint the exact problem a reader faces and then offer the solution. In general, these campaigns can feel very aggressive, but you should not let that deter you: You are offering something of value to the people who need it. The email just serves as a way to show those prospects how badly they need what you have to offer.

- **Long-term authority campaigns** work differently. Instead of building toward a sale, these act over time to build your authority within your niche. These campaigns consist of valuable content that informs readers and offers free solutions to their problems. In exchange, you build your credibility in your niche. In the long term, this strategy pays off in the form of prospects who become loyal to your brand and your message. They might refer you to their friends and colleagues, or they might be more likely to seek you out for help in the future. You can also use your authority as leverage for things like reviews that will boost your product's visibility.

- **Hybrid campaigns,** as the name suggests, blend elements of both strategies. Striking the right balance between them is something that you may need to experiment with, as it will differ from one campaign to the next. In general, the benefit of the hybrid model is that it allows you to build up your trustworthiness and authority while still driving sales in a more direct manner.

Consider the needs of your business and construct your marketing campaign accordingly. You may find that your needs change over time, and that's fine. You can always adjust your methods in order to create the perfect campaign for your present circumstances. In fact, making these adjustments is something I would encourage you to do, and I will cover it in greater detail further on in this chapter. For now, though, do some brainstorming about your immediate needs and goals, and build your initial campaign around those answers. It will save you a lot of trouble when you start sitting down to write content if you know what the purpose of that content will be.

> *It will save you a lot of trouble when you start sitting down to write content if you know what the purpose of that content will be.*

Understanding SPAM Laws

Before looking at the specific details of building a mailing list, it is important to discuss the legality of email marketing. A body of laws called the CAN-SPAM act was enacted in 2003, primarily to put limits on the practices of email marketers. You will want to follow the rules and guidelines established by CAN-SPAM both to stay within the boundaries of the law and to avoid aggravating your prospects. People want to sign up for your mailing list because they will receive valuable content in return or because they believe that you can provide relevant solutions to their problems. They do not want their inboxes filled with unwanted material.

Here is what you need to know:

- Your contact information needs to be accurate and accessible. This means that your name and business address will appear in your message as a way of verifying your identity. This information will be filled out automatically by any email delivery system, which I will address more in a later section.

- Subject lines need to accurately reflect the content of the message. They should not be misleading. In other words, you cannot send out a message with the subject line, "Regarding our last conversation..." if you have never spoken to the person before. You can't say "You have won $1 million" just to entice readers to click.

- Readers need to be able to opt out of messages. The opt-out information must be clearly spelled out within the body of the email itself. This, too, will be added automatically to your message by any good email management program.
- If a reader does opt out of the list, his request should be honored promptly. If you're using an email management program, this should be handled automatically, so it's not something you will need to concern yourself with too much.
- Your email should remind readers how they came to be on your list. A simple message stating, "You are receiving this email because you signed up at such-and-such website" should be sufficient. Again, this is something that you can use an email management program to display automatically in every message that you send.
- The email addresses that you gather should be used only for your own promotional purchases. You should not sell your mailing list to another party or use it for any other purpose.

As you can see, most of these regulations are straightforward and common sense. Simply using a reputable email management program will take care of most of these regulations for you.

Attracting Subscribers

Having a great series of emails lined up to be sent will not help you if there is no one to receive them. The cornerstone of any successful email marketing campaign is your mailing list, and building the mailing list requires you to attract and keep subscribers.

> *Having a great series of emails lined up to be sent will not help you if there is no one to receive them.*

Fortunately, attracting subscribers is not difficult. All you really need is a single webpage, called a landing page, that will attract the attention of people looking for more information in your niche. Then, you need an incentive for people to sign up. This is referred to in some circles as the "lead magnet," but it is really just the free content that you give away through your newsletter.

The Landing Page

A landing page can exist on its own or be part of your larger website. Landing pages get their name because they are often the first contact a person has with your brand. When searching for a particular topic or problem, the reader will "land" on your page. If the content of the page is good enough, and your initial offer is enticing enough, they will stay long enough to give you their email address. The number of times a person subscribes to your newsletter after landing on the page is called a conversion rate, and later I will address some ways you can monitor and improve it. For now, let's focus on what a landing page should include:

- **A powerful, attention-grabbing headline.** People who see your page should immediately be able to read the headline and think, "Yes, this applies to me." Because you know what problems your prospects face, you should be able to craft a headline that will speak to the very heart of those problems.

- Brief, upbeat text that excites readers and motivates them to get more help. The landing page is the single most important piece of content you can put on the Web. Take some time to ensure that the message and its delivery are spot-on. You will want to focus on active, enticing language and short, skimmable paragraphs. The goal is not to sound salesy or aggressive, but it should inspire action. You want the reader thinking, "Yes, this is exactly how I feel; tell me more!"

- **A personal touch.** Many landing pages include videos, which can be a great way to make an immediate connection with your visitors. By using your own voice or image on the page, you provide a real human connection between your content and the visitor. Your page does not need to have a video to succeed, but it certainly can't hurt to include one to really drive the message home.

- **Graphics.** The page should be visually interesting but

uncluttered. You will also want to include an image of the lead magnet. Even if the lead magnet is just a series of emails, create a graphical representation of it for your page. This makes the lead magnet seem more enticing and valuable.

- **Your credentials.** You need this landing page to establish you as a trustworthy source of information. This is a good place to talk briefly about your credentials and expertise so that visitors know your information will be valuable. If you have testimonials or endorsements, post a few here to grab a visitor's attention and boost your credibility.
- Most importantly, your landing page should have a sign-up form to gather the email addresses of your interested prospects.

You do not want to give away too much information on your landing page. The goal of your content here is to pique readers' interest and encourage them to sign up for the mailing list in order to hear more. You will want to spend time assessing the problem, speaking directly to your readers' needs, and then making a promise that you can help with that problem through your lead magnet.

Your landing page needs to be clean and functional, but it does not need to be fancy. In fact, having an overly slick presentation might actually turn away some prospects. You can hire a web designer to build this page for you, or you can create it yourself with a template and WYSIWYG (what you see is what you get) site-building tool. To find a simple landing page template, all you have to do is search; there are many available. Landing pages are also sometimes referred to as "squeeze pages," so you might find more templates and examples by using that term in your searching.

Before writing a landing page, it can help to look at examples from other people both inside and outside your niche. A quick search for "best landing pages" will lead you to several stand-out examples. You could also just put yourself in the shoes of your prospects and do a few web searches for the kinds of questions they would be most likely to ask. Doing this will inevitably lead you to landing pages for competitors in your niche, and you can be inspired by what they do well and make changes to the areas they need to improve when you build your own page.

> *The last thing you want is to create a landing page where important elements will be hidden from viewers simply because their computer is different from yours.*

Keep Your Design Accessible

Your landing page should be easily accessible to as many visitors as possible. This means, first and foremost, that it should be mobile-friendly. Most site builders offer the ability to craft a mobile version of your site. Do this, and test the site on a variety of devices, such as smartphones, tablets, and PC monitors of different sizes. The last thing you want is to create a landing page where important elements will be hidden from viewers simply because their computer is different from yours.

Another thing to consider is the growing popularity of ad-blocking programs. Some marketers still swear by pop-ups or splash pages as a way to grab the attention of visitors and usher them toward the sign-up form. While this can be valuable, it can also backfire if your users are running a program that will block your pop-ups. If you do choose to use any of these more intrusive tactics, do not put any vital information in them that would cripple your marketing if it were blocked. You do not want visitors to miss your sign-up form because it existed only in an ad-type widget that was blocked by their computer.

Don't Forget to Say Thank You

In addition to a landing page, you will also want to create a thank-you page. Visitors will be directed to this page after opting into your mailing list. The purpose of the thank you is twofold. First, it lays the foundation for the personal relationship you will be building through your mailings. Second, it gives you the chance to prepare your readers for what they can expect.

For example, the thank-you page can tell them when they can expect their lead magnet incentive to arrive. It will let them know what kind of emails they might get and reassure them that their information will not be redistributed. It can also clue them in on whether there are any additional steps to take, such as confirming their subscription.

Your thank-you page does not need to be fancy, and it's fine if it is sparse on text. As long as it's functional and sets the right tone for your interactions, you're fine.

Since the purpose of the landing page is to entice visitors to sign up for your mailing list, you will need to make your lead magnet attention-grabbing.

The Lead Magnet

Since the purpose of the landing page is to entice visitors to sign up for your mailing list, you will need to make your lead magnet attention-grabbing. This is the product that answers the "What's in it for me?" question that your visitors will be subconsciously asking. Ultimately, your landing page offers a value exchange: You are trading your lead magnet for their email address. Therefore, you will need to offer something valuable.

"Valuable" in this case does not necessarily refer to monetary value, although that is an option that some businesses might try. For example, a company might offer a free sample or short trial period to entice prospects to try the product and put them in line to receive further communication. You do not have to go this route, though, if it is not right for your business. If your niche is in solving people's problems, your lead magnet can be something as simple as a report or guide that will provide solutions.

For example, imagine that you are a consultant. Your lead magnet could be a guide providing detailed advice for solving one of the problems your clients frequently encounter. People looking for a consultant in any given field will probably be very interested to get that information, and it can provide a gateway for additional consulting work down the line if the reader likes your message and wants more information.

Other lead magnets could include ebooks, podcasts, videos, or any other multimedia if you wished. It could take the form of an online course or series of lectures on a given topic done in whatever formats you prefer. Ultimately, as long as the lead magnet offers value and fits with your overall message and marketing goals, the sky is the limit.

A Word on Automation

I will offer one word of advice on the topic of lead magnets: Whatever you choose, be sure that it is something that can be fully automated. In other words, it's fine to offer a free ebook that can be automatically delivered to the reader. It will not work, however, to offer a free phone consultation to everyone who signs up.

The reason for this should be obvious: You will not have the time to respond individually to every request for information. If you have done your job right with your landing page, you should get a heavy amount of traffic to your site. Dozens, hundreds, or even thousands of people might opt in to your mailing list. If you try to offer customized content to every single one of them, you will quickly burn out and fall behind.

The thing that makes your mailing list so valuable is that it largely maintains itself. It allows you to stay in contact with a large number of interested prospects without having to talk to each person individually. Embrace automation, and save your valuable face time for those prospects who are ready to pay you for your services.

Email Management Systems

The key to good automation is using an email management program. This service will provide the form that you post on your landing page for collecting email addresses. It will also gather and store those emails and allow you to craft the message for your campaigns.

Depending on the service you use, you may have a variety of options at your disposal for how those emails are delivered and what they look like. For example, you can set up some messages to send out automatically to anyone who subscribes. You can also set up time parameters, allowing certain messages to be sent at regular intervals or at a predetermined time, which lets you schedule as many emails in advance as you'd like.

There are a number of programs available. These are a few of the most popular:

- Infusionsoft
- Aweber
- MailChimp
- Email Delivered
- Constant Contact

Many more are available if you want to compare features and do some research. I personally prefer Infusionsoft, but you might want to look at the differences between various providers until you find one that suits your tastes. Regardless of which service you use, be sure to get acquainted with it and test out the features before making your mailing list available to the public.

Crafting Your Message

Once you have your landing page built and a good mail delivery system in place, it's time to start writing some emails. The first bit of content

> *Once you have your landing page built and a good mail delivery system in place, it's time to start writing some emails.*

that you will want to create is the lead magnet. Since this is the first introduction that anyone on your mailing list will have to your brand, you will want to be sure that it sets the stage for future messages. This means it should have a consistent tone with the other content you plan to provide. From there, all future emails should follow suit.

For example, if a company uses a free sample as a lead magnet, additional emails might provide information about upcoming sales or additional freebies as they become available. If your lead magnet is an in-depth guide about solving a particular problem, future emails might provide additional advice on that issue or on related concerns faced by people within that niche. Your emails do not all need to be closely tied to your lead magnet, but it will help if most of them follow the example you first set.

The content you create will also depend on the type of campaign you plan to use. If you are looking to build a short-term revenue strategy, your emails will focus on introducing a problem and pointing readers toward your paid solution. If you are going for a more long-term authority approach, your emails should give high-value information that will build trust among your readers.

Every email you send will generally fall into one of the following categories:

- Brief, high-value messages. These cut to the chase in 500 words or fewer. They quickly introduce or expound upon a problem and offer a solution.

- Exclusive content or deals that are available only to subscribers.
- Personality insights that give a little bit of background into your life or experiences and how they tie into your niche. These are helpful to add some meat to your long-term authority campaigns.
- Rallying your subscribers to an action that will help your business, such as leaving a review or "liking" your Facebook page.
- Longer sales messages that go in-depth in addressing a problem and providing a solution for fixing it.

There are a few variations on each type, but in general, every message you send will conform to one or more of these categories.

The Anatomy of a Good Marketing Message

If you have never written marketing materials before, it pays to spend some time practicing the format until you have it mastered. Every marketing message that you send will follow the same basic format:

1. Begin by introducing a prob-lem. This should be something

If you have never written marketing materials before, it pays to spend some time practicing the format until you have it mastered.

that your audience is familiar with and struggles with. This is the problem that you will be solving with your product or service.

2. Spend some time illustrating the problem. You might draw on your own life experiences to provide examples or simply delve more deeply into the experiences of people facing the issue. In either case, you will want to build up the problem to create a crisis in the mind of the reader. You do this by showing just how big the problem is and how important it is to solve it. Your goal here is to encourage the reader to realize, "I need to solve this right away."

3. Next, you will want to offer some solutions. You may do this in the bulk of the message if you're crafting an informative long-term authority campaign. If your goal is short-term revenue, you'll want to pitch your solution as being whatever paid option you provide. When doing this, be sure to make it clear how your product or service will solve the problem that you've described.

4. Finally, and most importantly, your message needs to end with a call to action. Now that you have presented a problem in the mind of your readers, it's important that they know what to do next. Your call to action can be anything from "Visit my blog to learn more" to "Call me for a consultation," but it needs to be present

in any marketing message.

This four-step process is the backbone of all marketing communication. Depending on your campaign, you may have some emails that deviate from this format, but the majority of your messages should still include these ingredients. Remember: You are a problem solver, and your role is to identify the issues your prospects face and to provide solutions. That is how messages are converted to sales, and it's why email marketing campaigns are so effective.

Setting Up an Autoresponder

As we discussed earlier, automation is a crucial component of a successful email marketing campaign. One of the greatest perks of this type of marketing is that you only have to invest time into creating content once. After you have written the emails, you can use them indefinitely with no additional effort on your part.

To keep things running smoothly, you will want to use an auto-responder. This is a function that is included in any good email management program. The first auto-responder you set up might be the one for your lead magnet: Every person who signs up for the mailing list will receive an email or series of emails delivered automatically. These emails are triggered when a new contact is added to the mailing list, and they will be delivered at whatever intervals you set up.

For example, let's say that you entice your visitors to sign

up for your list by offering a three-part course on a particular topic. The visitor signs up for the course, and within
minutes receives the first email. A few days later, the next
email arrives. The third email follows a few days after that.
Every person who signs up will receive the same email series with the same amount of time between messages.

You can use the auto-responder for your existing
contacts as well. For example, imagine that you run a
pest-control company. You might want to send a message
with tips for handling mosquitoes during the summer and
another about bed bugs in the winter. By setting these up
automatically, your content will arrive in the inboxes of all
of your subscribers every year at the appropriate time.

The Three-Email Sales Series

If you are planning to use a short-term revenue campaign,
building it around a series of auto-responder messages clustered in groups of three is a very successful method. Here is
what the campaign looks like in practice:

1. Begin with an email giving a detailed overview of a
   specific problem, then close the email by telling your
   reader that you will address this problem more in-
   depth in the next message and provide solutions. This
   lays down the groundwork for the three-email campaign and piques the reader's interest.

2. Schedule the second email for two to three days after
   the first. In the second email, focus on building up the

"crisis" aspect of the problem. Explore the problem thoroughly and make it clear that a solution is necessary. Close this email with a promise that the next message will provide the solution.

3. The final email, delivered within a few days, should quickly recap the issue brought up in the first two messages, and then provide an overview of your solution. Finish it with a call to action encouraging your reader to buy your product or call you for a consultation.

Each three-email cluster should take no more than a week to resolve. After a few weeks or months, you can send out another similar campaign on a different topic or problem. The purpose of the three-email cluster is to really drive home your message while boosting your readers' engagement and excitement. The anticipation of your next email will leave prospects feeling more interested in seeing it through to its conclusion, much like the cliffhanger ending to a good TV show.

Don't Forget Broadcast Messages

Although the auto-responder is a powerful tool, it should not be your only method of delivering a message to your subscribers. You should also utilize broadcast messages to provide timely information and prevent your newsletter from sounding too "canned" or impersonal.

A broadcast message is one that you send manually

rather than schedule automatically. You might write it just before sending it, or you might have several prewritten messages ready to send out for certain circumstances. If you are not writing these from scratch, you will still want to take a couple of minutes to look over your prewritten message and tweak it as necessary to ensure that it is up-to-date, personal, and relevant.

There are several reasons why you might send a broadcast message:

- You have released a new product and want to alert your readers.
- You are asking for a specific action, such as a review or Facebook "like."
- You are offering a special promotional opportunity to your subscribers.
- You have made a change in your business, such as expanding your offerings or changing your services.
- You want to update your readers about an important milestone.

Generally, you should view your broadcast messages as alerts or "breaking news" about your business. Providing this sort of timely update breathes life into a campaign and reminds your subscribers that there is a real person behind the emails. It can also generate immediate action, especially if most of your auto-responder campaign is geared toward building up your credentials, authority, and trust. After spending so much time getting to know your brand, your readers will be eager to act on your requests.

Tips for Successful Marketing Campaigns

Now that I have covered the basics of establishing your email marketing campaign, it is time to look at a few tips and tricks for getting the best value for your time:

- Set up your list so that new members receive content more frequently than people who have been subscribed for a long time. You can do this through carefully managing the settings of your auto-responder messages. You will want to hook new subscribers with lots of high-quality content early to ensure they stick around. People who have been subscribed for a longer time will be happy with more occasional updates.

- Spend time thinking up compelling subject lines. This is the only part of your email that a subscriber is guaranteed to see, and it needs to be catchy and interesting to entice the prospect to open it and read it.

- If you are doing a long-term authority campaign, liven up your content by offering it in a variety of formats. For example, do a combination of "Top 10" style lists, personal anecdotes, or surprising facts, in addition to more straightforward informational pieces.

- Design your messages with short paragraphs and plenty of white space. This makes them faster and easier to read, which in turn makes reading your emails more enticing. Remember that you are competing against many other things that subscribers could be doing with their time, so make it easy for them to engage with your content.

- Avoid the urge to create fancy-looking HTML email templates. Plain text is easy to read and doesn't feel overly polished or spammy. Many readers will not turn on HTML in their emails anyway, so your brilliant formatting will go unnoticed. Keep it simple, and focus on the message.

- Proofread your emails and try to maintain good spelling and grammar throughout. You do not have to be perfect, but obvious errors will make you seem unprofessional and can be jarring for readers.

> *For a marketing tool to be truly successful, you will need to pay attention to the performance of your list and make changes as necessary to improve your results.*

Metrics and Measurements: Are You on the Right Track?

Setting up an email campaign and creating content for it is only the first step. For a marketing tool to be truly successful, you will need to pay attention to the performance of your list and make changes as necessary to improve your results. This involves gathering information about your subscribers and their behaviors, and then using these metrics to modify your approach.

There are several things you will want to be able to track when running an email campaign:

- Are the emails effective? Are they leading to personal interaction with your subscribers? Are your sales increasing?
- Do your emails have a high opening rate, or are they sitting unopened in people's inboxes?
- Are people unsubscribing frequently or staying on the list?
- Is your landing page effectively converting visitors into subscribers?

Fortunately, there are easy ways to track all these metrics.

The first should be straightforward. You should be able to see these results directly. If your sales go up after an email campaign, it's reasonable to assume that the two events are related. If people are acting on your calls to action, then you know your message is effective.

Your email management program can also provide you with valuable information regarding the performance of your campaign. You will be able to see what percentage of your emails are opened and track this data over time and for any given email. This allows you to see which campaigns are most effective and spot useful trends. For example, you may notice that certain subject lines result in more opened emails than others; this means that you should use similar subject lines in the future and avoid those that led to fewer clicks.

When it comes to tracking the effectiveness of your landing page, measuring performance becomes a bit more complicated. There are a few things you can do to see how well your page is performing:

- Look at the statistics of the page itself. Your webhosting program most likely provides you with statistics about how many visitors you have attracted and how long those visitors stay on your page. If you see that your number of visitors is much higher than your number of new subscribers, it could be a sign that something about your landing page is not working.

- Test this theory by creating two versions of your landing page. You can use software like Google's "Content Experiments" to keep two versions of the page running. When a visitor arrives at your site, he will get one of the two available versions, and you can track the performance of each version through the analytics page of the Content Experiment program.

- Alternatively, you can simply change the page and compare the new version with the last one. This is a simpler method, but the information you gather may not be as thorough.

- Regardless of which method you choose, focus on

modifying key elements of your page. Try changing the headline, modifying the text or updating the layout. For best results, make one change at a time and give it a few weeks so that you can gather the results of your experiment.

- Also consider changing your email opt-in form. Some people find that a form requiring only an email address results in higher conversions than one asking for both a name and an email.

- You can also try changing your lead magnet if you are dissatisfied with your results. Your offer may not be enticing enough to earn the number and quality of subscribers that you want. Before you do this, however, be sure that you have thoroughly tested the landing page first. It is much easier to tweak the text of a single webpage than to come up with a completely new incentive for your visitors.

Monitoring the performance of your landing page and email campaign is an ongoing job. You will want to use these metrics to guide the development of future content and modify your approach to improve your results. This is all part of engaging with your prospects, and its importance to your overall business goals should not be overlooked.

Are Your Emails Being Delivered?

Bear in mind that even if your message is perfectly compliant with the CAN-SPAM laws, it can still be caught in the spam filter of a reader's email inbox. Many major email providers are very sensitive toward unsolicited emails, and this can lead to your messages going astray.

One way to prevent this is to set up your mailing list with a double opt-in. This means that your readers will need to confirm their subscription before they are added to the list. Usually this takes place immediately after inputting their email address in the form on your landing page. When they go to their email, they will find a message requesting confirmation; inside that message will be a link they'll need to click.

This does add an extra step to the opt-in process, and you may lose some conversions along the way. However, you will greatly reduce your odds of having your messages marked as spam by readers who forgot that they had ever signed up in the first place.

Going Forward

In today's Internet-obsessed world, inbound marketing is more powerful than ever. People go to search engines with their problems and questions, and they are eager to seek the help of experts who can offer real solutions to those concerns. For the prospects in your niche, finding your landing page can be like the answer to a prayer. This makes email marketing a mutually beneficial arrangement: You offer quality content and solutions, and in return they give you a captive audience for your brand's message.

Starting your own email marketing campaign is not diffi-cult. Following the steps I outlined in this chapter will get you up and running right away. Over time, you will need to review your campaign's performance and make changes, but the ongoing effort you put into this project is low compared to the value these prospects bring to the table. As a business owner, there is nothing more effective than personally en-gaging with the people who are most interested in what you have to offer. Email marketing can bridge that gap to bring you closer than ever to your prospects.

6 SOCIAL MEDIA

S ocial media is a game-changer for marketing. In the past, a brand could only communicate with its target audience by broadcasting a message through large channels. Now, you can form a personal relationship with your audience, cultivating your message to get closer to your prospects and building reciprocity. The most effective marketers today use social media to stay relevant and keep up with trends in the industry while constantly paying attention to the needs of their audience.

The most effective marketers today use social media to stay relevant and keep up with trends in the industry while constantly paying attention to the needs of their audience.

I am not referring to Facebook ads and sponsored posts, although these these tools can also be very valuable. What I'm concerned about is using social media the way it was intended: As a tool for connecting with people and sharing information. Used correctly, social media becomes the most powerful free marketing resource at your disposal. What other marketing channel out there allows you unfettered access to millions of potential fans?

While you may already realize the importance of social media, you might be overwhelmed at the prospect of building an online platform from the ground up. There are so many social media sites, each with their own unique quirks, that building a web presence can be daunting. Fortunately, there are a few strategies and "best practices" that you can put to work to boost the effectiveness of your social media campaigns. By setting up a platform for your brand, you can boost the signal for your message and drive traffic back to your blog; in turn, you will see your prospect pool growing and enjoy a boost in sales.

Building a Platform

The process of developing an online presence is called "building a platform," and it is one of the most important things you can do to stand out in a crowded marketplace. There are several reasons why your platform becomes integral to your brand:

- It boosts your authority in a given topic by showcasing your knowledge.

- It helps you to become more accessible to people who are interested in learning more about what you have to offer.
- It facilitates communication with your audience and helps to leave a lasting impression with your prospects.
- It heightens your reach, allowing you to send your marketing message to a wider audience than you could otherwise reach.

Once your social media presence is established, you will quickly find that a personalized approach is the most effective way to grow your influence. Even better, building a social media presence can actually be a lot of fun, and there are a few tools that can help you automate parts of the process and free up some of your time. Once your audience begins to grow, you may find that interacting with them is the most enjoyable part of your marketing strategy.

> *Once your social media presence is established, you will quickly find that a personalized approach is the most effective way to grow your influence.*

Understanding Different Social Media Sites

Although it is easy to think of "social media" as a whole, the truth is that "social media" is a catchall term for a very diverse set of websites. Every social media site has its own

culture, with certain types of content being more readily shared and certain conventions being more common
Learning how the biggest social media sites work is the key
to tailoring your approach and getting the best results from
your efforts.

Twitter

Twitter came onto the scene in 2006 and quickly exploded
in popularity, particularly among celebrities, businesses,
and other busy people who need to stay visible to their
audience without investing a lot of time creating content.
Twitter revolves around 140-character messages, or tweets,
that can be linked together through the use of hashtags.
These hashtags are words preceded by the pound sign (#)
that act like keywords in a blog: Clicking a hashtag will take
you to a feed showing every other tweet that includes that
same hashtag.

Twitter is an extremely popular social media outlet for
marketing and platform building because the built-in expectations of fellow members are different than on a site
like Facebook. On Twitter, you have followers rather than
friends. In practice, this means that people are more likely
to follow anyone who seems interesting, allowing an account to amass a huge quantity of followers.

Twitter Tips

- Follow people in your niche. Most people on Twitter follow back, so the fastest way to grow your audience is to follow others in your niche.
- Post frequently, but don't flood your feed. Aim for about six tweets per day.
- Vary the type and content of your tweets. Alternate between posting tips, linking to articles, making comments about what you're working on, for example, to keep the feed interesting.
- Pay attention to the quality of the accounts you follow. Do not follow people who are spammy, don't have their own avatar pictures, or have few followers themselves. Always follow people more successful than you so that you can rise to their level.
- Be generous about retweeting, linking, publicly commending people, and otherwise being social and cooperative.

Facebook

Facebook was launched in 2004, but it took a few years for it to change from a social hang-out for college students into the massively influential website it is today. Now, Facebook has become practically synonymous with social media, and a person's Facebook profile is really their online persona. Businesses absolutely must join Facebook today in order to stay relevant in the market.

Unlike Twitter, where you fire off short bursts of information and have ongoing conversations with your followers, Facebook is a lot more like a miniature blog. You can post longer chunks of content in addition to images, videos, and links, and you can foster a conversation in the comments section of each post. This makes Facebook more intuitive for bloggers, and it also helps to foster a sense of community around your brand.

Facebook Tips

- Decide whether you want a page or an account for your brand. Some people can benefit from having both a professional Facebook account, which can friend other users, and a page, which can gain followers.

- Do not be afraid to share some personal details from time to time on your professional page, but don't go overboard. Save the photos of your kids and rants about your day for your private Facebook account.

- Facebook thrives on sharing. Try to gear most of your posts around either a link or an image that can be shared. Turn your tips into images rather than posting them as bald text; it will boost the number of shares you get and encourage virality.

- Remember, not everyone who is following you will see every post you make. The more likes, shares, and comments you get from a given person, the more of your updates that person will see. Encourage your followers to interact with your posts.

LinkedIn

While other social media sites were designed to keep friends and family in touch with each other and then later co-opted by businesses, LinkedIn's primary purpose has always been professional networking. The site actually launched back in 2003 but remained largely under the radar until recently.

On LinkedIn, one of the most valuable things you can do is join groups related to your niche. These groups act like dedicated forums, allowing you to communicate with others who share your interests. This will broaden your range, since otherwise you can only add connections to your LinkedIn profile if you already have a relationship with them.

LinkedIn Tips

- The atmosphere of LinkedIn is more professional and less personal. Keep your posts relevant to the interests of the people in your network, focusing on the "What's in it for me?" message.
- LinkedIn primarily shines in a B2B atmosphere. If you are selling a product or service to another professional, you will do well on LinkedIn. The site is not the best

choice for a company that sells to basic consumers.

- Read the rules of any group you join to be sure that sharing links is allowed before posting. In most cases, though, you should have no issues with sharing your content as long as it is relevant to the topic at hand.
- Use your LinkedIn as a resume or CV to showcase your achievements.

Google Plus

Google+ is one of the newest social media sites. Google had high hopes for its network, which acts alongside the search engine and email programs to boost the effectiveness of both, but the site's popularity has been sluggish. There are not as many people spending time on Google+ as on other social media sites, and the Google Authorship program failed to take hold the way some people expected.

However, there is one definite advantage to Google+ over other social media sites: You can use it like a light version of your mailing list. If you use Gmail, it is very easy to add everyone in your contacts to Google+. This allows you to unobtrusively keep tabs on everyone you've worked with in the past. It is also very easy to automatically cross-post your blog updates to Google+, and you can also incorporate Google+ into your comment section to link the site with your blog with minimal effort.

Google Plus Tips

- Google+ is a smaller network and should not be your primary focus; use it as a secondary backup to your main social media campaign.
- Harvest contacts from your Gmail to stay in touch with colleagues and clients.
- Because Google+ is smaller, feeds tend to be slower. Don't worry about posting throughout the day; just update your Google+ feed when you have something relevant to share, such as a new blog post.

Other Social Media Sites

The above four sites are valuable for businesses, but they are not the only ones out there. Depending on your brand's values and your overall marketing strategy, you might find that your message will be better served by another site. For example, Pinterest and Instagram have a large following and are a great venue for image-based marketing techniques. If your brand has a story that can be told through images rather than text, one of these sites might work better for you. Once you get the basics of social media marketing down, start experimenting to see what works for your brand.

Keeping It "Social"

Although social media is a valuable marketing tool, it would be a mistake to think of it purely in terms of marketing. In fact, trying to use your social media account as a way of blatantly pushing sales will have the opposite effect: Your fans will become annoyed and dissipate, leaving you alone like the unpopular guy crashing an office party. You do not want to chase off your potential prospects by coming on too strong.

Social media is first and foremost a way to connect with people.

Social media is first and foremost a way to connect with people. You are not broadcasting a message into the ether like a television commercial. You are interacting with real individuals, who have their own opinions and tastes, and your success depends on how well these interactions go. Think of social media as a giant virtual cocktail party. You are there to network and build connections, certainly, but you are also there to relate to people and have a good time. Nobody likes to spend time with the person who won't stop talking about himself, so you need to focus on making your social media message useful and interesting to the people in your audience.

Stop thinking about selling things or boosting traffic to your website. In fact, although it might seem counter intuitive, stop thinking about building a platform at all. Instead, think about what kinds of people would be interested in what you have to say, and determine what you can offer those people that would be valuable. High-quality content will keep your readers around, encourage sharing, and attract new subscribers. By focusing on quality above all, everything else will fall into place.

Your Social Platform Is Not Your Virtual Home

There is one important thing to remember about building a platform: Your social media profile is not your home base on the Internet. Your brand cannot get by on social media accounts alone. In order to really benefit from social media marketing, you need your own website or blog to act as the command hub for all your other online activity. Everything else you do on the Internet should act as a pathway to lead people back to your main site.

With that in mind, be careful not to spend too much of your time and energy on social media until you are ready to profit from it. A web presence is vital, but it will not help you if your website is not monetized effectively or if you do not have strong products to offer. Before you start building your platform, be sure that you have something of value to give

> *... be careful not to spend too much of your time and energy on social media until you are ready to profit from it.*

to the visitors who see you on social media and want to learn more about your brand.

General Tips for Social Media Tactics

I described a few of the social media sites above and explored what makes them different from each other and what tips can help you excel in any given site. Now, I want to give you a few general tips that will make your social media experience more successful across every site you join:

- Use a profile picture that shows your smile. Having your face on all your social media interactions will add a human element to your brand and boost your authority.
- Fill out your profile or "about" page with relevant information about your business, and be sure to link it back to your main website or blog.
- Do not use a social media autoresponder. Some parts of social media can be automated, but you should always keep personal interactions authentic.
- Focus on the quality of your subscribers rather than the quantity. A handful of very active and engaged readers is better than thousands of followers who tune out what you say.
- Take the time to build up your web presence authentically. Do not try to rush the process, and do not fall back on any cheats or gimmicks; you will be penalized in the long run.

Vary Post Types for Best Results

You do not want to bore your followers by posting the same

types of content all the time. Your social media account should not be a dumping ground for links to your blog and nothing more. Vary your posting types to build a solid connection with your audience and maximize the effectiveness of your platform:

- Share tips or insights that people in your niche would be interested in hearing about. Use images, especially on Facebook, to make these tips more shareable.
- Post links to your own blog posts and articles.
- Post links to other people's blog posts and articles that are relevant to your brand. Retweet interesting tweets from other people in your niche. Foster a sense of community and shared resources.
- Send shout-outs to people in your niche who have achieved something or would be interesting to your followers. Twitter has #FF "Follow Friday," which allows you to recommend people for your subscribers to follow.
- Keep people updated on your current projects. Post announcements about your achievements and let people get a sneak peek at in-progress projects. This helps your audience feel more involved in whatever you are working on.
- Share some personal information or insights. Do not do this often or overshare, but let people get a glimpse into your personal life from time to time to help you seem

more human. A good example would be mentioning a vacation you just returned from or a restaurant you enjoyed visiting.

- Provide discounts and special offers. People who subscribe to your social network platforms generally expect to get added perks. Make social media–exclusive special offers or discounts for your products.

It's best to brainstorm a large number of posts in advance so that you always have a pool of them to draw from. Try to think up 50 to 100 posts of all imaginable types and keep them saved somewhere. Use these when you are struggling for content or can't think of anything new to post. After a while, you can even reuse some of the same content to repost your best tips, but try to avoid this; focus on keeping things fresh so your readers will stay engaged.

Driving Traffic to Your Site

Having a strong social media presence on its own will not help you much. Having a solid platform without a well-monetized site to promote is like renting a kiosk in a shopping mall without having goods to stock it with.

In order to benefit from your social media efforts, you will need to use the social media account to drive traffic toward your blog. By far the easiest way to do this is to post links to your blog onto your social media sites. In order to do this effectively, though, you will need to pay attention to two important elements: your headline and your summary.

Making Tweetable Headlines

When you are writing a blog post, think carefully about your headline. You will want a title that is keyword-focused, enticing, and easy to share. Pick something short enough that you can tweet the entire title, plus a relevant hashtag or two, and still leave room for someone to retweet it. That will maximize your visibility on Twitter and make it easier for people to share your information.

Enticing Summaries to Gain Clicks

On Twitter, all you have is an engaging headline and some hashtags to get the point across. On other sites, you have a bit more room. Make the most of it by posting a brief summary or teaser on your Facebook, LinkedIn, or Google+ wall before linking to the blog post. A bald link seems spammy and will not entice many clicks, but an attractive link with an image and some enticing text will incite curiosity and drive traffic toward your site.

Programs to Boost Efficiency

Keeping up with the diverse needs of several social media accounts can feel exhausting, but there are a few programs that can make updating your feeds simpler:

- HootSuite: This must-have program allows you to manage multiple social media accounts from within a single app. You can schedule upcoming tweets and posts in advance, allowing you to map out your posts through out the day without needing to update your feeds manually.

- Buffer: This Google add-on allows you to quickly tweet from any page and link to the content that you've found. It is very helpful when browsing the Internet to be able to link to a useful site or tweet about it without needing to open Twitter to do it. Think of Buffer as Twitter's answer to the Pinterest Pin-It button.
- SocialBro: This program is a must-have tool for identifying and measuring the behaviors of your audience. It lets you see who is following you and enables you to spy on their reading habits so that you can modify your strategy accordingly.

By writing posts in advance and scheduling them to post automatically, you can free up a lot of your time. Just do not rely on automation too much; you will still want to pop in from time to time to answer questions and communicate with your followers.

How to Maximize Social Media Traffic

Just as it takes time to build up a blog following, your social media platform will not burst into life overnight. However, focusing your efforts on building high-quality content and weaving together all your social media activities will help to grow your network. Here are a few additional tips for driving traffic to your social media profile:

- Let everyone know about it. Put your Twitter handle on your business cards and email signatures. Be sure that there are links to your social media accounts on your website. Add a Twitter feed to your blog. Let people know that you're on social media and how to find you.
- Ask for people to follow you. Never underestimate the power of a strong call to action. Use one social media account to send followers to another with a post like "Find me on Twitter for more updates" or "Like me on Facebook for special offers."
- Post regularly without spamming, and pay attention to the site you are using. Tweeting six times a day is totally acceptable, but six Google+ posts would be excessive. Look at the frequency of posts among other people in your niche and follow suit.
- Ask for retweets or shares on your most powerful tips or best ideas.
- Do not stop friending people and expanding your influence.

Once you have captured the attention of your audience, they will start promoting your work for you through shares, likes, comments, retweets, and more.

Try to follow 50 new people every day on Twitter, and constantly join new groups on LinkedIn to widen your network.

Once you have captured the attention of your audience, they will start promoting your work for you through shares, likes, comments, retweets, and more. This is why social media is the key to viral marketing, and it's the most powerful method imaginable for building trust and authority for your brand.

7 RETARGETING

The goal of marketing is to bring people to your business and, ultimately, to buy your product or service. For web businesses, this usually means driving traffic to your site and converting the visitors into buyers. With this in mind, it becomes important to make sure that every visitor to your site is given ample opportunities to convert.

The problem with a linear conversion model is that it does not reflect the way that most people shop. The standard marketing approach involves attracting a customer through the use of targeted keywords or advertisements, then enticing that buyer with content on the webpage. Unfortunately

> *The goal of marketing is to bring people to your business and, ultimately, to buy your product or service.*

for marketers, most people do not settle for the first product they find when shopping. Instead, they usually want to mull over the purchase and compare the product to its competition before making up their minds.

During that process, it is crucial for a business to keep its brand visible to the potential buyer. Otherwise, you run the risk of fading from the buyer's mind. His search might have taken him to your site initially, but he may have forgotten all about your product by the time he decided to make a purchase.

Fortunately, there is a solution to this problem that is easy to implement and ubiquitous in Internet marketing: Retargeting. In fact, this technique is so common that another company is probably retargeting you right now. Despite its popularity, though, many business owners still do not participate in retargeting or know how to get the most out of it.

In this chapter, I will address what retargeting is, how it works, and why it has an excellent ROI compared to other types of advertising. I will also go over some of the common pitfalls that marketers might fall into when implementing a retargeting campaign and provide some tips about how to avoid these issues.

What is Retargeting?

Retargeting is such an integral part of the Internet that you probably encounter it every day without paying much attention to it. For example, let's say that you have been thinking of taking a trip to Hawaii this summer. You travel to Google and search for information about travel costs for different dates. Later, you notice that there are advertisements for flights to Hawaii popping up on other websites that you visit throughout the day.

Retargeting is the mechanism that makes this possible. It's what controls whether you see certain advertisements, and it is responsible for the sudden influx of certain ads after you have performed various actions online.

From a marketing point of view, the purpose of retargeting is to lure back visitors who have gotten partway toward making a purchase but have not yet converted. Visitors who browse an online store without buying anything can be retargeted; so can web searchers who type certain keywords into search engines but do not buy the products associated with those keywords.

Retargeting is valuable to marketers because the recipients of retargeting are already one step closer to converting. When you retarget a visitor who has previously looked at your product, you know that he is already interested in your products—or at least aware of your brand. This removes some of the hurdles you face when you are marketing to new customers who have never heard of your brand or who may not necessarily be looking for what you sell. This is why, on average, retargeting campaigns are more successful than other types of ads in terms of their ROI. It is also why implementing a retargeting campaign is so crucial to your business.

How Retargeting Works

Retargeting works through the use of browser cookies. A cookie is a line of code that a website uses and a browser temporarily stores when a person visits a particular website. It is used to anonymously track the behavior of the visitor, allowing the browser to "remember" a visitor's past behavior.

When a person visits a website that utilizes retargeting, a cookie is delivered. This allows the site to recognize the visitor if he or she returns at a later date. It also works on other sites that host ads for the initial site. When the visitor stops off at one of these sites, the cookie will inform the site of the visitor's previous behavior. This will then trigger behavior specific to the visitor's browsing history.

For example, say that you run an online clothing store. A person visits your site but doesn't buy anything. Her browser will pick up a cookie. Later, when she gets on Facebook, her browser sees the cookie, letting Facebook know about her behavior. At this point, if you have a retargeting campaign set up, your campaign will bid in real time for the chance to display an ad. If you win this bid, your ad will display when the visitor loads the page.

All of this happens within a fraction of a second, and the process is fully automated through the retargeting campaign manager. In order to make it work, all you need to do is establish your campaign, provide all the relevant ads and set a daily budget for the campaign. I will go into this process in more detail later; first, let's explore the three main types of retargeting campaigns that can be used by marketers.

Types of Retargeting Campaigns

The basics of retargeting are the same for all campaigns: In every case, your retargeting system will use cookies to anonymously track a visitor's behavior and display customized ads related to that behavior. However, the behavior being tracked and the location of the advertisements will vary depending on the type of campaign you run. Depending on your needs, you may find that one option works better than another; you may also discover that you get the best results by combining multiple campaign types to maximize your visibility.

Website Retargeting

A website retargeting campaign uses cookies to track a visitor's behavior on your own website. There are two ways this might work. The first is for ads located throughout the web, such as on social media. The other is for ads within your own site.

For example, imagine that you run an online department store. A user browses your store, looking at a pair of designer blue jeans, but does not buy them. The next time that user visits, your site might display an ad for those same jeans, gently prompting the visitor to remember how much she wanted them and encourage a sale. This can squeeze a conversion out of an interested visitor.

With website retargeting, the user picks up a cookie from your website. You achieve this by putting a small line of code, called a pixel, within your site's design. The pixel is what triggers the browser to pick up or drop a cookie, and it helps your campaign management program observe the behavior of the campaign for analytic purposes.

Search Engine Retargeting

It is likely that your online business already utilizes search engine marketing in order to drive traffic to your site. You can use a similar approach for retargeting. In this case, the behavior you are targeting is a person typing in a particular keyword into the search. This will trigger a cookie, which later will communicate that behavior to a site where ads for your site can be run.

So, for example, imagine that a user is searching online for information about camping equipment. You own a site that sells tents and other camping gear. When the user types in a search string related to what you sell, his browser will pick up a cookie. Later, when he checks his email, he might see an ad at the top of the screen for your website. This is search engine retargeting, and it can be very powerful when run alongside your other advertising campaigns.

When setting up a search engine retargeting campaign,

you might find that it is more effective to target slightly different keywords than those you use for per-click ads. This is to widen your prospects and prevent any single user from being unnecessarily inundated with your ad while searching.

Email Retargeting

Email retargeting is one of the most powerful tools at your disposal because it requires very little action on behalf of your prospects. You probably already have a mailing list established for your business in order to stay in contact with prospects. An email retargeting campaign marks your mailing list subscribers with a cookie, which will then trigger an ad under the right circumstances, such as visiting your website or browsing social media.

You can experiment with the settings of your marketing campaign to determine what action will cause the subscriber to be retargeted. For example, you could retarget everyone on your mailing list, or you could retarget only those subscribers who read your newsletter without clicking the links inside. This allows you to squeeze the maximum value from your mailing list and gently urge some of your more reluctant subscribers into converting.

How Do You Set Up a Retargeting Campaign?

Your retargeting campaign is managed by a provider. This provider will create the code that you place on your website, and it will secure you potential advertising space on certain websites. The bidding for space in any given advertising area is handled automatically, so once the system is in place it should essentially run itself.

Many companies offer retargeting campaigns. You may already be using a company that offers retargeting services. Google, for example, offers retargeting as part of its AdWords program. There are several other well-known companies that specialize in retargeting as well:

- Adroll
- Fetchbank
- Retargeter
- Chango

Aside from these well-known groups, you may be able to obtain retargeting services from another advertising company. It is a good idea to compare multiple providers before settling on one, as features, benefits, and costs can vary between companies.

DIY or Managed Option?

Most ad companies will give you the option of running your own campaign manually or choosing a full-service managed option. The full-service option will naturally cost more money, but it is usually the better bet if you can afford it. This is because a good retargeting campaign can be complex, and tracking all the relevant information by hand and solving problems as they arise can be very time-consuming.

Look carefully at your budget and determine if it would be feasible to go with a managed option. If not, learn as much as you can about retargeting and the technology behind it so that you will more fully understand what's going on with your campaign.

Regardless of whether you opt for a DIY route or choose a fully managed option, be sure that you keep track of as much analytic information about the campaign as possible. By seeing which ads are converting well and what type of visitors are most likely to convert, you can better modify your campaign to target exactly the people you are most interested in drawing back toward your brand.

Tips for Success

Now that you know how retargeting works and have a general idea of what types of retargeting campaigns you can use, here are a few tips that will help ensure success:

- Avoid showing too many impressions. The point of retargeting is to gently prompt your prospects into action or to keep your brand in the forefront of a user's mind. If you have too many impressions, you will come off as spammy or desperate, and the visitor may begin to tune out your message entirely. A good rate is to display an ad to any given retargeted user no more than once every other day or about 15 times per month.

- At the same time, be sure that you are showing enough impressions. It is easy to get shy about bombarding your readers, and you might hesitate to get your message out there. Don't worry about coming off as "stalkerish"; retargeting is so common online that Web users run into it every day and likely do not even realize what's happening. Again, aim for an impression once every other day until your prospect converts.

- Be sure that you have good ads to run. Since you need to bid for ad space to show your retargeted ads, the ads need to be worthwhile. This means they should be attractive and engaging enough to capture a viewer's attention and drive a conversion. Study successful advertisements in your niche to create something that will stand out.

- Be careful when retargeting customers who have already converted. The primary purpose of retargeting is to capture additional conversions from people who would otherwise have left your site without doing anything. If you serve ads to people who have already purchased your product, you run the risk of alienating your buyers by bombarding them with sales messages. Only retarget your existing customers if you have something of value to offer. For example, you can tag a buyer with a cookie so that you can display an ad for a future sale or a loyalty reward. To do this, you just drop a pixel into your "Thank You" page.

- As tempting as it might be to maximize your presence, never use more than one retargeting program at a time. This is because for any given impression, your ad will bid against others for viewing space on a particular website. If you have multiple providers, you will end up bidding against yourself and driving up your costs unnecessarily. Stick with one provider at a time, and only switch if the results are not what you are expecting.
- Be sure to segment your campaign wherever it makes sense. In other words, brainstorm specific goals for specific pages. Your retargeting campaign will be most effective when the ads served to visitors are highly relevant to their previous behavior. Visitors who view a product should receive a different message from those who have subscribed to your mailing list or searched for a particular term.
- Measure your results and modify your campaigns accordingly. Analytics are a key part of marketing. By monitoring the performance of your campaign, you will be able to see what works and what doesn't work so that you can make changes accordingly.

Make Retargeting Work for You

Retargeting is a major part of marketing for e-commerce companies, but it has its place in many other industries as well. A B2B company, for example, could utilize these same strategies to keep its products in the forefront of a potential client's mind during the sales cycle. Even a university could benefit from retargeting as a way to boost enrollment numbers among interested students.

Any business or organization can benefit from retargeting as a way to recapture the interest of prospects that may otherwise have walked away from the offer without a second thought. Once you understand the basics, you can find countless ways to incorporate retargeting into your overall marketing plan.

8 DIGITAL MARKETING ANALYTICS

There is one key difference between a successful b usiness and one that never gets off the ground: Marketing. Without attracting customers, your digital business is dead in the water. But simply drawing new customers in is not enough; you need to understand what those customers are thinking and how they are interacting with your brand. This is where analytics comes into play.

In many ways, marketing is like science. In a scientific study, you would make some guesses, test them, and then use that data to modify your approach going forward. Marketing endeavors are exactly the same. It is not enough to simply create a marketing campaign and turn it loose in

A good marketer knows that the best campaigns are those that are constantly being improved.

the wild: A good marketer knows that the best campaigns are those that are constantly being improved.

In order to make improvements, you need to be able to accurately see how you are performing. This means that you need a marketing campaign with results that are measurable and specific. You also need a way to review these measures, or metrics, and analyze them to determine what they really say about your efforts. Fortunately, there are a number of analytic tools at your disposal to keep track of your progress. It could be as simple as identifying your metrics and selecting the right tool for the job.

In this chapter, I will delve into what metrics you should keep track of and suggest some tools for monitoring them. Afterward, I will go into more detail about what exactly you can do with all this information and how you can use your knowledge to boost the effectiveness of your marketing endeavors.

The Marketing Cycle

> *Marketing is a constant process. It never stops.*

Marketing is a constant process. It never stops. It does, however, move in a cyclical pattern, allowing you to learn from the past and apply what you learn to the future as you come back around to the same process:

- Begin by identifying the target audience of your marketing campaign.

- Look at your competition and see what they are doing so you can compete.
- Identify where your audience can be found, whether online or off, so you can target your marketing appropriately.
- Set measurable goals for your campaign.
- Develop a strategy for meeting those goals.
- Put your strategy to work.
- Measure your results.
- Analyze those results so you can put that knowledge toward your next marketing campaign.

As you can see, measuring and analyzing your results is a crucial part of the cycle. Without that analysis, you will not be able to make the changes to add value to your marketing endeavors, and your results will begin to stagnate. Only by learning from the past can you make the right changes to improve the future.

What Should You Measure?

Marketing involves many moving pieces. In any given marketing campaign, there could be a lot of variables affecting your end results. Below are some common metrics clustered by type. The more of these metrics you can track, measure, and analyze, the more thorough your results will be. Just be aware that no single metric will tell the whole story. For a really accurate snapshot of your campaign, you will need to gather as much information as possible from each category below.

Organic Search and Property Performance

These metrics all look at the quality of your website in terms of organic search results and the site's overall strength. Organic results are especially important to track because they give you insight into how well your search engine optimization is working: If you are getting a lot of unique visitors, that's a sign that you are ranking well for keywords that people are searching for.

Unique Visitors

This is one of the simplest things to measure: How many new people are coming to your site each day?

Unique Visitors Seven-Day Trend

This builds on the above. By looking at your trend over the duration of a week, you can see whether your traffic is growing, dropping, or maintaining consistent levels. This also helps you see how your traffic might spike when you add new content to a site, giving you an idea of how well a new blog post or page is working.

Bounce Rate

The visitors you attract are not helpful if they do not stick around long enough to offer any helpful or even constructive suggestions. Bounce rate measures how frequently someone lands on your page only to navigate away from it. A bounce can be caused by many things, but there are two common contenders. First, the site may fail to deliver what the visitor is looking for. This can happen if the keywords you are targeting with your SEO are not a good match for the rest of your content: A reader looking for how to cook steak is not going to stay on a site that is predominately about classic cars. The other reason a reader will bounce is if the site is poorly designed, difficult to navigate, or just does not seem to offer quality content. If you have a high bounce rate, it's a sign that something about the design or SEO of your site needs to be changed.

Average Time on Site

When readers stay on your site, that is a sign that they are engaging with the content. You want long stays. The more time your readers spend looking at your pages, reading blog posts, or watching videos, the more of a connection they will have with your brand. This means that each reader will be much more likely to become a conversion later. If you have a low bounce rate but viewers are not spending much time on the site, it is probably a sign that you are not offering enough content to keep the reader engaged.

> *When readers stay on your site, that is a sign that they are engaging with the content.*

30-Day Change in Google Rank for Target Key Phrase

Keyword searches can fluctuate hugely from day to day, and a single-day snapshot of your Google rank will not tell you much. To see how you are really doing for a specific keyword, you will need to look at the overall picture for the month. A 30-day glimpse at your Google rank will tell you how you are doing for your keywords and phrases and let you know if there is a problem with your SEO strategy.

Domain Authority

Domain authority is actually a combination of other metrics compiled to determine how well your domain will likely place within Google searches. High-authority sites are those that rank highly in search engines. Each individual page in your site has a page authority as well, separate from your domain authority.

Of course, just because your site gets a lot of traffic does not mean that it is going to be successful at converting that traffic into profit. You will need other metrics to let you know whether the audience you've attracted is really the right target for your marketing.

Advertisement Performance

Organic search results are golden, but they are often not enough to drive the traffic and results you need. This is where advertising budgets come into play. If you are placing ads on

Facebook, Google, Bing, or any other venue, you need to know that your marketing dollars are well spent. Here are a few metrics you should keep in mind when designing and monitoring your ad campaign:

Total Reach

The total reach of your ad is, quite simply, how many people have the opportunity to see it. Your reach is often determined by the amount of money you spend, but being careful with your choice of targeting can help you boost your reach by pinpointing a receptive audience that may not have as high a level of competition.

Click-Through Rate (CTR)

The click-through rate, or CTR, is a record of how many people clicked on your ad after viewing it. If you have a high reach but a low CTR, it's a sign that either the ad itself is not working or the product you are offering is not enticing enough to capture a viewer's attention.

Cost Per Lead

The cost per lead is one way to track the efficiency of your advertising strategy. To get your cost per lead figure, you will need to take the amount you've spent on a campaign and divide it by the number of leads it generated. You will ideally want to target this in such a way that only leads from that campaign are measured. This will give you a good idea of whether your ads are converting customers or not.

Cost Per Sale

The cost per sale is similar to the metric above, except that you are tracking actual sales rather than leads. In businesses that are built on long relationships and communication, leads are very valuable. For other businesses, focusing purely on sales is a better indicator of how profitable a campaign has actually been. In either case, tracking the cost per sale or lead will give you an idea of whether your advertising costs were worth the results.

Email

Email is one of the most powerful tools at your disposal for connecting with your prospects. If prospects go so far as signing up for your mailing list, you know that they are interested in your message. This is why it is important to monitor the performance of your email campaigns to ensure that you're getting the results you want.

Open Rate

This rate measures how many of your emails are actually opened rather than left sitting discarded in a reader's inbox. If you have a low open rate, most likely it is because your subject line failed to intrigue the reader or the email landed in a spam filter rather than the recipient's inbox. A low open rate is a sign that you need to pay more attention to your subject lines

Email CTR

Emails, like ads, can have a click-through rate. This applies in any case where your email nudges a reader toward taking an action, whether it's visiting your website, watching a video, or going to your sales page. If you have a low CTR for your emails, it may be because your call to action is not compelling enough.

Email Engagement Rate

Engagement is a tricky thing to pin down. When it comes to your emails, engagement mostly means that a person opens and reads the message. Therefore, your engagement rate will be closely tied to your open rate. The difference between opening and engagement is that engagement happens over time whereas open rates look at each individual email. So an engagement rating allows you to look at the behavior of readers over a span of time to see whether the same people are continuing to open and read emails. If you are reaching new audiences or losing old ones, you will spot it in your engagement statistics.

Social Media

Social media is a relatively new channel for connecting with your audience, and it can be hard to see exactly how it fits into your overall marketing picture. Just as print and digital marketing can sometimes target different audiences, you might find that the people interacting with your Facebook feed are not the same as those on your blog. This makes tracking your social media activity all the more important.

Social Engagement Rate

Engagement on social media is easier to track than in other areas because it is much more active. Instead of passively reading, social media followers can like, share, or comment on any piece of content. Keeping track of all this activity can help give you an overall picture of how active your fans are. Just do not get too hung up on this figure: An active, engaged group of followers is great, but it does not translate directly to a successful business.

Virality Score

Virality is one of the most sought-after qualities of online content. It is also the hardest to measure or even define. Basically, viral content is content that takes a life of its own; it's a message that your readers pass along for you. For example, consider a commercial. A standard commercial is played on a network to the audience. A viral commercial is one whose audience shares the ad with all their friends. You want to go viral because it means your message will be spread far wider than it otherwise could.

To measure virality, most people rely on the k-factor. Your k-factor is the way to track exponential growth: How many extra people will you get for each person you attract on your own? Some people debate the effectiveness of k-factors and others suggest that it is impossible to really measure virality at all, but keeping an eye on these metrics can at least help you get some idea of whether your content is going viral.

Conversions

A conversion occurs whenever a person takes an action. This means that a conversion could be a sale, but it could also be a phone call, blog comment, or email address submission. Any time a person visits your page and takes action based on what he sees there, it counts as a conversion.

> ... *a conversion could be a sale, but it could also be a phone call, blog comment, or email address submission.*

Since conversions are ultimately at the heart of your profits, your conversion rate is a very important metric to monitor.

<u>Landing and Sale Page Conversion Rate</u>

You will have separate conversion rates for every sale page and landing page you own, because each of these pages will have its own call to action. Tracking conversions is as simple as dividing the number of people who opted into the offer on that page by the number of visits a page receives. This will show you how effective a page is at converting visitors into prospects or prospects into sales.

Total Cost per Lead

I addressed cost per sale as it relates to advertising several pages above. Your cost per lead is a more all-encompassing figure. It takes into account every marketing dollar spent across all your activities, divided by every lead you have converted. This gives you an idea of how efficient your marketing activities are.

What Analytics System Should You Use?

Because there are so many metrics to measure when it comes to a marketing campaign, you will need to use several programs to analyze your data. Fortunately, a handful of programs can handle most of your needs automatically.

If you are going to get serious about monitoring your marketing data, you will want to look into getting these programs:

- Google Analytics. The gold standard for analytics measurements, this program will track your website for visitors, bounce rate, stickiness, and more. If you are opposed to Google for some reason, there are a few other open-source programs that do most of the same things. Check with your web host to see what options are available.

- A mail management system. A program like Mailchimp or Constant Contact will allow you to send newsletters, but it will also offer tons of analytics about those mailing lists. This is the program that will track your conversion rate for newsletter sign-ups as well as click-through rate, engagement, and more.

- Analytics for your ads on Facebook, Google, Bing, etc. These ad companies have their own analytics program that can be used to monitor how well your ad campaigns are doing and how engaged your prospects are.
- Social media monitoring tools. Facebook has some built-in monitoring capabilities for pages, but you might want the extended capabilities of more thorough multichannel social media analytic tools like Social Report.

Analyzing Your Data

Of course, simply gathering data is not enough. You also have to put what you have learned to good use. After all, information is useless if it is not analyzed. So once you have gathered some data, it is time to sit down with your information and pay attention to the big picture. Do not get too hung up on the details of any single metric or any particular day. Look instead at trends, and see what you can glean from that information. Here are some examples of things to review:

> *... information is useless if it is not analyzed. So once you have gathered some data, it is time to sit down with your information and pay attention to the big picture..*

- Bounce rate. Are people leaving your site because the content is not what they expect? Or are they leaving because it is displayed poorly or the layout is hard to navigate?
- Conversion rate. Are you getting plenty of conversions? Could you get better conversions by changing your incentive, tweaking the wording of your call-to-action, redesigning your page, or anything else?
- Ads. Are you reaching the right audience? Would you get a better click-through rate if the ad were reworded or targeted to a different demographic? Is the cost of the ad worth the value of the lead?
- Engagement. Once you attract visitors, what are they doing? Are they sharing your content? Are they sticking around to read more information? Are they signing up for your newsletter? If not, how can you encourage them to do those things?

As you explore your data, make notes of things that seem to stand out, such as a low conversion rate or a high bounce rate. Then start brainstorming some ways you might be able to improve them. This will help you develop a split-testing strategy.

Split Testing: The Scientific Method for Markets

There is a simple reason why your marketing goals need to be measurable: You need to be able to test them. If you choose metrics that are easily measured, you will be able to run several versions of a campaign and test them against each other to see which one works the best. When you do this, your original data will serve as the "control" of the test you're running; all the new versions are variables.

Split testing can be performed on anything. For example, you might decide to run two different ads on the same channel to see if one is more effective than the other, or you might run the same ad on two different channels. These two tests will help you see whether it is your ad itself or your target demographic that is affecting your results; this information you can then use to modify your approach in the future. When testing, pick a single variable to test at a time. Otherwise, you will not know for sure which of your changes was effective.

Here are a few types of split tests you can run:

- Develop two versions of your landing page and set them up so that visitors will randomly land on one or the other. This will let you know if your landing page itself is the issue behind your conversion rate, or if there is another problem. After you have tried a few landing pages, try two versions of the same page with different incentives. If more people sign up for a free video than an ebook, for example, you know which incentive your demographic prefers.

- If you are having trouble with your bounce rate, consider tweaking your SEO strategy and testing the new version of the site.

- Run the same ads across multiple channels to see which areas attract the most attention from your target market.
- Try sending different emails to different sections of your list. You can divide up your mailing list according to various criteria from within your mail management program, and this will let you test out new headlines, message types, and more.

As you can see, nearly any metric imaginable can be isolated and tested. Once you have some practice with split-testing, you will realize that it is often possible to pinpoint the exact variables affecting your results. While making the changes needed to improve those results is not always simple, the metrics make it a whole lot easier to get started.

Putting the Information to Use

There is a popular saying among marketers: "If it can be measured, it can be improved." Your job as a marketer is never complete because there are always ways to improve your results. Even if you are happy with your current sales numbers, you can always find ways to grow your company, and seeking growth is a good thing. This growth is what will allow your business to stay competitive and continue adapting to the challenges thrown your way.

Once you have identified your areas for growth and tested some solutions, you should be able to draw valuable conclusions from those results. You might realize that you have been targeting the wrong demographic, or maybe some part of your message was not being communicated clearly. Once you isolate and solve this problem, you should be able to set new goals and start the cycle again.

One of the most valuable uses of marketing metrics is determining the cost-benefit analysis of your marketing activities. Without a clear image of which parts of your marketing are effective and how much each lead or conversion is really costing you, you have no idea whether your marketing budget is sufficient. Having metrics on your side makes it easier to tell whether you need to spend more on advertising, hire better talent, or trim a bloated budget to widen your profit margins.

Ultimately, taking a shot in the dark is never the right move when it comes to marketing. A successful campaign requires a well-thought-out approach. Take the time to develop a strategy, set some measurable goals, and build an action plan for achieving those goals. By monitoring your results, isolating variables, and testing your solutions, you can ensure the best possible results.

9 UPSELLING

Upselling is a sales technique whereby a seller induces the customer to purchase more expensive items, upgrades, or other add-ons in an attempt to make a more profitable sale.

Upselling usually involves marketing more profitable services or products, but it can be simply exposing the customer to other options that were perhaps not considered. (A different technique is cross-selling in which a seller tries to sell something else.) In practice, large businesses usually combine upselling and cross-selling to maximize profit. In doing so, an organization must ensure that its relationship with the client is solid. Upselling depends on a trust relationship with a happy customer.

Probably the best-known example of upselling is the McDonald's sales technique of asking "Would you like fries with that?" It's simple, it compliments the original purchase decision, and it works. McDonald's earns 18 cents on a $2.09 burger sale, and $1.14 extra profit on a fries and Coke upsell! The upsell profit is 6.33 times the core product profit.

> *Upselling is recommended. Customers want to buy from people who know more about products than they do.*

Upselling is recommended. Customers want to buy from people who know more about products than they do. The goal for any company is to let the customer know how they can easily make their experience much better by buying additional products.

So how do you do this exactly? It all comes down to product definition.

Initially, you start out with one core product, one engagement product and a lead magnet. Unless your core product is a consumable or recurring, there needs to be another core product related to the initial core product that you can sell to your customer. During the upsell, you would initially propose a high margin product or service to your core product customer. If this offer is not accepted, you offer a different, albeit related, core product to this customer.

As your business grows, you will continue to add high margin products and core products so that you have a portfolio of goods and services that directly benefit your customer.

It is this method, Upselling, that turns one time customers in to lifetime customers.

Conclusion
MOVING FORWARD

Throughout this book, I have tried to highlight the importance of high-quality content and white hat SEO practices. I have done this not because I'm a stickler for the rules but because these practices work. I have seen positive results time and again in my own businesses and in those of my clients, and I am confident that, if you implement the strategies I have presented in this guide, you will also see success.

A successful digitally marketed business is not something that happens on its own, and it is not something that you can create overnight. However, as I hope you have seen from what I have presented in

> *A successful digitally marketed business is not something that happens on its own, and it is not something that you can create overnight.*

this book, setting up a high-quality site and promoting it is not as difficult as you might expect. With a little know-how and the proper tools, you will be able to turn your passion into reality—a high-earning site that captures the attention of visitors and converts them into paying customers eager to put money in your pocket each and every day.

Of course, none of us truly knows what the future holds. A few years ago, the Internet was a very different place, and successful businesses used different strategies in order to succeed. Social media has been a game-changer. Blogging has become more sophisticated and will continue to evolve. In a few years, digital marketing may be very different than it is today, but I am confident that the basic ideas I have outlined in this book will serve you well in the changing landscape of Internet marketing.

The exact details of your marketing strategy can and will change as your business grows and technology evolves. New apps and new software will hit the market, streamlining your automation or analytics. New social media sites will appear, new niches will open up, and audience expectations will change as a new generation of shoppers enters the marketplace.

Despite all these changes, however, a few things will always remain the same: People will always need high-quality content, and they will always do business with companies they trust. That is what makes the content first marketing approach I present in this book so powerful. Building your business on a solid foundation of great content ensures that it will remain strong no matter what happens in the virtual world.

More than that, I have tried in this book to teach you a little bit about the psychology of great marketing and show you the ideas that underline each of the techniques I have presented. This should arm you with the knowledge to make smart choices in the future as you keep up with the rapidly changing world. By teaching you the "why" in addition to the "how," I hope that I have prepared you to tackle any marketing challenge you may encounter head-on.

For More Information . . .

Although this book is a rather thorough reference of many marketing concepts, it is obviously not possible to cram everything you need to know about digital marketing into a single slim guide. Once you have reviewed this book and mastered its concepts, you are probably going to be hungry for more. Or, perhaps, you may still be a little confused or uneasy about some part of the marketing process—or you may just need some help actualizing your dreams.

Whatever the case, I can help. My company, Clear Again Media, specializes in finding innovative ways to engage with your online audience, whoever and wherever that may be. We can help your business reach its goals and provide personal guidance for building the strength of your marketing campaign. To learn more about what we can do for you, visit our website at http://ContentFirst.Marketing.

THANK YOU FOR READING

I truly hope that you have enjoyed this book and that you are able to put these ideas to work right away to grow your business. If you have learned something from this book, I would love to hear from you! Feel free to contact me at john@ContentFirst.Marketing with any questions or comments.

You can also subscribe to my newsletter (http://contentfirst.marketing/contact-us/) for more great content like this. Also, don't forget to stop in at my website (http://ContentFirst.Marketing/TheBook) for more and information and free bonuses.

ABOUT THE AUTHOR

John Arnott is a leading authority on digital marketing and media. For the past 20 years, Mr Arnott has built marketing and sales efforts around digital channels.

As the CEO of Clear Again Media, Mr. Arnott has launched countless product sites and has invested heavily in continual testing of what works when marketing online.

John lives in Dallas, Texas, with his wife and two daughters.

http://www.ClearAgainMedia.com

CPSIA information can be obtained
at www.ICGtesting.com
Printed in the USA
FSHW021952040820
72688FS